THE ULTIMATE ENCYCLOPEDIA OF

KNOTS
& ROPEWORK

THE ULTIMATE ENCYCLOPEDIA OF
KNOTS
& ROPEWORK

GEOFFREY BUDWORTH

southwater

This edition is published by Southwater,
an imprint of Anness Publishing Ltd,
Blaby Road, Wigston, Leicestershire LE18 4SE;
info@anness.com

www.southwaterbooks.com; www.annesspublishing.com

If you like the images in this book and would like to investigate using them for
publishing, promotions or advertising, please visit our website
www.practicalpictures.com for more information.

A CIP catalogue record for this book is available from the British Library.

Publisher: Joanna Lorenz
Project Editor: Sarah Duffin
Designer: Michael Morey
Photographer: Rodney Forte
Production Controller: Wendy Lawson

PUBLISHER'S NOTE
Although the advice and information in this book are believed to be accurate and
true at the time of going to press, neither the authors nor the publisher can accept
any legal responsibility or liability for any errors or omissions that may have been
made nor for any inaccuracies nor for any loss, harm or injury that comes about
from following instructions or advice in this book.

CAUTION
Do not use any of the knots, bends, hitches, etc. in this book for a purpose that
involves foreseeable risk of loss, damage or injury without the appropriate training and
equipment. Cavers, climbers, rescue workers, wilderness or ocean-going adventurers
who wish to use a particular knot for those (or any other) activities and pursuits are
strongly advised to seek the advice of qualified practitioners first. This book is intended
only to be a safe and simple introduction to knot tying.

Contents

INTRODUCTION

*"It is extraordinary how little the average individual knows about the art
of making even the simplest knots."*

(R.M. ABRAHAM – *WINTER NIGHTS' ENTERTAINMENTS*, 1932)

Knotting is an enjoyable pastime. Most people can learn to tie knots and soon acquire an
impressive repertoire. Knot tying is as absorbing as reading a good book, and the end product
is as satisfactory as a completed crossword or jigsaw puzzle – but with many more practical
applications. Everyone ought to know a few knots; that is why the International Guild of
Knot Tyers (IGKT), founded in 1982, is now a recognized educational charity. Nobody should
be over-dependent upon safety pins and superglues, patent zips (zippers) and clips and other
fastenings, when a suitable length of cord and the right combination of knots are cheaper,
consume less of the planet's scarce energy resources and often work better.

There are several thousand individual knots and an almost infinite number of variations of
some of them. In addition, new knots emerge every year from the fingers of innovative knot
tyers to increase the existing numbers. Then there are the ornamental aspects: macramé;
leather-braiding and whipmaking; Chinese decorative knotting; Japanese *kumihimo* and other
elaborate braiding or plaiting techniques; traditional British corn dollies; tassels, tatting and
crocheting. Magicians and escapologists practise knot and rope trickery. Mathematicians
venture into three dimensions when they explore the abstruse topological field of knot theory.
For periodic dabblers and serious devotees alike, knotting is a delightful pursuit, a lifelong
obsession, and for a few fortunate individuals it is a wonderful way to make a living. This
book cannot possibly cover everything outlined above, but the 200 or so carefully chosen
knots it contains will gently challenge those new to knot tying and, it is hoped, even teach
more experienced hands a thing or two.

KEY TO KNOT USER GROUPS

Angling/Fishing

Boating/Sailing

Caving/Climbing

General Purpose

Outdoor Pursuits

History, Origins and Uses

Cave dwellers tied knots. The 1960s American knotting writer, Cyrus Lawrence Day, believed that knots pre-dated (perhaps by several millennia) the time when humankind learned to use fire and cultivate the soil, invented the wheel and harnessed the wind. Unfortunately, any tangible evidence for this has long ago decomposed, but the first knotted materials are likely to have been vines, sinews and raw-hide strips from animal carcasses. There are some credible clues from non-perishable artefacts dug up by archaeologists that humans used knots and cordage more than 300,000 years ago. However, there is nothing to indicate what knots were employed before the earliest surviving specimens, less than 10,000 years old – fragments of nets, fishing lines, amulets and clothes – found in prehistoric garbage dumps and with mummified bog bodies. So we know that Neolithic folk tied the overhand knot and half hitch, reef

✦ ABOVE
The artful geometry of rope.

✦ BELOW
Codline and water-resistant coir contrast with darkly tarred and weatherproofed, aromatic hemp hawsers and spun yarn.

the time human history was first
recorded, the artful geometry of
rope was already established,
inherited from a prehistoric time
beyond the memories of the
oldest and wisest scribes.

KNOT LORE

Knotted cords were used in
primitive cultures to keep track of
dates, events and genealogies; to
recount folk lore and legends; as
mnemonic memory cues in prayer
or confession, and to record
trading transactions and
inventories. Both the rosary and
the abacus probably evolved from
knotted cords. The Incas of
ancient Peru made ropes of
maguey, derived from the
tropical agave plants, that were

◆ BELOW
Old glass fishing floats are protected by
a network of meshes.

(square) knot, clove hitch and a
running noose – and probably
others too. They used them to
snare animals, catch fish, tote
loads, perhaps as surgical slings –
and to strangle the occasional
enemy or sacrificial offering. The
Late Stone Age lake-dwellers of
Switzerland were excellent
ropemakers and weavers, who
also used the mesh knot (similar
to a sheet bend) in their nets, and
they would have instantly
recognized the cord reticules that
secure and protect those glass
floats – now found in many
waterside cafes – which once
supported the gill or drift nets of
seagoing fishing fleets. Indeed, by

strong enough for the primitive suspension bridges they constructed over mountain chasms. They also produced excellent textiles, and their bureaucracy, lacking a written language, relied upon elaborate coloured and knotted fringes of cord known as *quipus* (Quechua: *quipu* = knot) to keep decimalized records and so administer an empire that extended 4,827 km (3,000 miles) from north to south.

In Hawaii, as recently as 1822, illiterate tax gatherers kept a comprehensive tally of what was collected from each and every inhabitant on the island, in cash or kind, by means of a cord over 800 metres (half a mile) long, to which were attached knots of various colours and materials – one representing dollars, another hogs, others indicating dogs, pieces of sandalwood, and so on.

Ancient Egyptian art tells us regrettably little about their

knots, but we know that they applied the theorem of the Greek mathematician Pythagoras (*c.* 580–500 BC) to solve practical surveying and building problems

by making 12 equal knotted intervals in a rope and then stretching it into a 3,4,5 triangle.

Even the legendary Gordian knot of ancient Greece is a

♦ ABOVE LEFT
A "pudding" fender.

♦ ABOVE RIGHT
A boat fender neatly enhanced with a cast-off length of machinery drive-belt in the centre.

♦ LEFT
Needle-hitched bottles or flasks, with a rigger's canvas tool bucket and a kitbag.

♦ OPPOSITE
A sailor's ornate chest becket or handle.

Whisk brushes, in progress and completed.

mystery. Gordius, father of Midas, was a peasant who rose to be king of Phrygia and – so the story goes – tied his by then redundant farm cart with leather harness traces and presented it to the temple of Zeus. So intricate was the knot that nobody could untie it, and the oracles proclaimed that whoever did so was destined to become emperor of all Asia. Alexander the Great tried his hand at this knotted puzzle but soon lost patience and, according to one account, severed it with his sword. "To cut the Gordian knot" came to mean disposing of any intractable problem at a stroke.

SAILORS AND COWBOYS
It is not necessary to like boats to enjoy knot tying. Indeed boating these days yields few opportunities to tie knots. It is equally wrong to assume that knot tying emerged only from sailing-ship crews. It is true that it flourished when

ropework evolved aboard the massive square-rigged warships and merchantmen of the 18th and 19th centuries when sailors had to cope with increasingly complex rigging. The sailor's chest becket or handle shows how seamen then turned in their leisure hours from practical to ornamental knotwork. This era lasted, however, for barely 150 years. Cowboys tied fancy knots and braids every bit as elaborate as those done by sailormen. Ashore,

knots had always been tools for those who engaged in particular trades and pursuits: archers and anglers, basketmakers, bellringers, bookbinders, builders and butchers, carters, cobblers and cowboys, dockers (longshoremen), falconers, farmers, firemen and fishermen, gunners, jewellers, millers, pedlars and poachers, riggers (in circus and theatre), shopkeepers, soldiers, steeplejacks, stevedores and surgeons, waggoners and weavers. There

◆ BOTTOM
Cargo-handling hooks for dockers (longshoremen) – or prostheses for disabled pirates.

◆ BELOW
A monkey's fist door-stop.

was a time when a handy whisk (brush) and maybe a chunky door-stop, both made from rope, could be found in many homes.

MYSTICS AND MEDICS

The practice of knotting is an ancient one. Knots were believed by some to possess supernatural properties and wizards and witches were known to have traded upon that fact. The legendary Greek epic poet Homer (traditionally a blind minstrel living in the 8th century BC) has Aeolus, king of the winds, give Odysseus a leather bag in which all of the winds are tied up.

The Greek philosopher Plato (c. 428–347 BC) detested the blacker aspects of knot magic and wrote, in his *Laws*, that those who preyed upon the gullible by

means of knot sorcery should be put to death. As recently as 1718, the Bordeaux parliament in France sentenced someone to be burnt alive for bewitching an entire family by means of magic knots.

In his *Natural History*, the Roman scientist and historian Pliny the Elder (AD 23–79) advised that wounds bound with a Hercules knot (a reef or square knot) healed more quickly. Indeed, those who learn first aid today still use this knot for slings and bandages but are unaware of the reason why.

Preserved in the medical collections of the 4th century AD Greek physician Oreibasius of

Antique hardwood fids, used to help tuck in the working ends of a knot.

Classic boat fenders of coir.

Pergamum are 18 knots, originally described three centuries earlier by Heraklas as surgeons' knots. These are regrettably not illustrated, but have been interpreted to include the overhand knot, reef (square) knot, the clove hitch, a noose, a fisherman's loop knot, the jug, jar or bottle sling, Tom Fool's knot, a cat's cradle, the true lover's knot, and – quite possibly – the constrictor knot.

An early, Scandinavian form of birth control, when a couple decided they had a large enough family, was to name the last-born boy Knut (meaning "knot"). In some places it was thought that a cure for warts was to tie knots in a piece of string, one knot for each wart, and then to discard the string; thereafter, the first person to contact the string would acquire the warts.

One of the earliest heraldic knots was the carrick bend used by the Saxon leader Hereward the Wake, who in 1071 AD revolted against William the Conqueror. In heraldry, it is still called the Wake knot.

Romantic allusions to the true lover's knot continually crop up in English literature after 1495 AD. Although there is no clue as to whether such a knot existed, several contemporary knots, with two interlocking identical parts, are referred to by that name.

CLASSIC KNOTS

Who invented or discovered all of these classic knots? Some of the simpler ones must have arisen spontaneously, in separate regions of the world, wherever somebody picked up a flexible bit of material and idly toyed with it. Then again, others are likely to have been spread by foreign traders and occupying armies. Imagine tracing a particular knot – say the distinctive jug, jar or bottle sling – from hand to hand and back through the centuries to its originator (an impossible notion, of course). History, as far as the activity of people was concerned, might have to be revised and rewritten.

Materials

Rope has been made by man since the Stone Age, utilising the materials that were available. European hunter-gatherers, 10,000 years ago, grew only one crop – flax – and that was for rope, not food; the ancient Egyptians and Persians made rope from papyrus and flax. Even a captive orang-utan is reported to have made a kind of rope from its bedding material and then swung from it.

It is no surprise that man has gone to such lengths to develop and enhance rope-making materials. Rope enabled humankind to probe the deepest caves and to seek fuel and ores in underground mines; to migrate over rugged terrain with pack animals; to capture, harness and ride other beasts; to sail and cross oceans in search of treasure, trade, conquest and colonization. Rope concentrated the efforts of the labour force that built the great Egyptian pyramids and created the blocks and tackles with which medieval European stone masons erected their Gothic cathedrals and castles.

VEGETABLE FIBRE CORDAGE
As we have seen, until this century, rope was made from the shredded, combed and graded fibres of plant stems such as flax and jute, or from the leaves of sisal and abaca (hemp). It was made from fibres attached to seeds (cotton), and from other vegetable materials as diverse as fibrous coconut shells (coir),

horse and camel (even human) hair, date palms, reeds, esparto grass, wool and silk.

Because of its origins in nature, such cordage is also referred to as natural fibre. These fibres were spun clockwise (or righthanded) to create long yarns. Several of these yarns were next twisted up anticlockwise (counterclockwise) into strands. Finally, three strands were laid up clockwise or righthanded which created a typical rope.

NATURAL ROPE

A lefthanded (or S-laid) cable consists of three righthanded (Z-laid) hawsers. Each of these ropes has three lefthanded (counterclockwise) strands made from numerous righthanded (clockwise) yarns, spun from vegetable fibres.

The incurably romantic – who wish that square-rigged sailing ships were still commonplace – regret the demise of these vegetable fibre ropes, with their evocative smells and every shade of gold and brown; but, with the emergence of synthetic (manmade) cordage, the shortcomings of natural fibre ropes became intolerable. They were comparatively weak, even when scaled up to enormous diameters. Unable to withstand

SYNTHETIC (MANMADE) ROPE

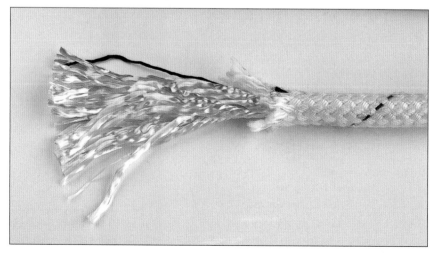

A 14 mm ($7/12$ in) diameter, soft matt polyester, 16-plait sheath encloses a hawser-laid core of several thousand high-tenacity polyester filaments.

◆ BELOW
Vegetable fibre knotted cordage in its natural element.

◆ BELOW
Natural fibre ropes vary in colour and may be blonde or brunette.

much abrasion, vegetable fibre cordage was also prey to mildew, rot, insects and vermin. It swelled when wet (so knots became impossible to untie) and froze in icy conditions with irreparable weakening as brittle fibres broke. Such ropes were also rough on the hands.

Obtainable only from specialized sources, and at a premium price, the use of natural fibre cordage is now very limited, – except in situations (such as filming a costume drama, rigging a classic wooden boat, and designing the interior decor and window dressing of nautical pubs, clubs and restaurants) where the appearance of an earlier period must be evoked. Some thoughtful

souls, however, concerned by what they perceive to be a profligate use of the earth's finite resources, prophesy an eventual return to natural fibre cordage, the raw materials of which can be harvested from renewable growing crops, without destructive ecological footprints.

Sisal rope is still sold for general purposes. Children shin up best-quality soft hemp ropes in school gyms. Coir is used for boat fenders. And for weather-resistant serving and seizing of wire and rope rigging by professional riggers, balls of tarred hemp spun yarn are still sold in several sizes.

It used to be that a rope could only be as long as the ropewalk (open field or long shed) where it

was made – although, of course, two or more could then be spliced together – but compact modern machinery has overcome this and, with extruded synthetic filaments, rope of practically any length can be made.

SYNTHETIC (MANMADE) CORDAGE

Discovered and developed by research chemists in the 1930s, the basic elements for synthetic cordage are: very fine continuous clusters of multifilaments, less than 50 microns/$\frac{1}{500}$ in across and of uniform diameter and circular cross-section; coarser monofilaments, individually more than 50 microns/$\frac{1}{500}$ in in diameter; discontinuous staple fibres (from

Terylene and Dacron); poly-propylene, which is best for mundane domestic use; polyethylene (or Polythene), often sold as balls of twine; and a few so-called "miracle fibres" (such as Kevlar, Dyneema or Spectra) representing the latest and more expensive cutting edge of ropemaking technology. There are two grades of nylon: Nylon 66, discovered in the Du Pont laboratories, was the first manmade fibre of merit available to the cordage industry, and Nylon 6, subsequently developed by I.G. Farbenindustrie. Terylene was a British development from investigations at the Calico Printers Association, the sole rights were then taken up by Imperial Chemical Industries.

2 cm/⅝ in to 2 m/2 yd in length) made by cutting multifilaments or monofilaments into discrete lengths; and flat, narrow, ribbon-like strings produced from extruded split or fibrillated film. The brightly coloured balls of twine often found in hardware shops and stores are usually split film products, as are the larger balls and cops (cylindrical reels) sold at garden centres for horticulture use or as baling twines for agricultural machinery.

All of these raw materials make cordage that is size-for-size stronger and lighter than its vegetable fibre equivalent. A three-strand nylon rope is more than twice as strong as a manila one, yet it weighs half as much and may last four to five times as long. Many can be dyed a variety of colours (even including psychedelic patterns). Almost as strong when wet, they have a high tensile (breaking) strength and are also able to withstand sudden shock loading. Although not plagued by the ills that afflict natural fibre ropes, they are more susceptible to heat generated by friction – softening, melting and even parting in extreme cases.

The most common manmade materials are: polyamide (nylon), the strongest man-made cordage; polyester (best known trade names

◆ RIGHT
Man-made cordage is smoother than
natural yarn, but stronger.

MANMADE MATERIALS

"MIRACLE FIBRES"

Kevlar – discovered by Du Pont as
long ago as 1965 – is an organic
polymer immune to moisture and
rot. Weight-for-weight it is twice as
strong as nylon, but with low
elasticity, and it has been used to
replace wire halyards. Then there is
Spectra or HMPE, the brand name of
Allied Chemicals who manufactured
this super-lightweight polyethylene
(marketed by others as Dyneema and
Admiral 2000). Its phenomenal
tensile strength is greater than that of
stainless steel. Released in 1985, it
looks set to supersede Kevlar. The
considerable cost of these will not
deter ocean yacht racers or climbers,
for whom competitive edge and extra
safety margins are worth any price,
but they are not recommended for
routine knot tying.

POLYAMIDE (NYLON)

Polyamide is the strongest manmade
cordage (although 10–15 per cent
less when wet) and cheaper than
polyester. It is very elastic, stretching
under a load anything from 10 per
cent to 40 per cent, then regaining its
original length when the load is
removed. This makes it suitable for
mooring lines, also towing and rock-
climbing ropes – but not in the
restricted space of caves or crowded
moorings, where stretchy ropes could
be a liability. It does not float, so
nylon can also be used for yachting
anchor warps. The best colour to
buy is white, as colouring may weaken
the fibres by 10 per cent (while

certainly adding a lot to the price).
A fairly high melting point of up to
260ºC (478ºF) ensures a reduced risk
of melting due to friction; but be
warned, it will, like all synthetics,
soften and be irredeemably weakened
at a much lower temperature than its
melting point. Polyamide withstands
attack from alkalis (and acids, to a
lesser degree), oils and organic
solvents. It has acceptable resistance
to photochemical degradation from
the ultra-violet wavelengths in
sunlight, and to abrasion. Domestic
consumers of this product will be
impressed to learn that it is
recommended for deep-sea towing
and widely used in the off-shore
oil industry.

POLYESTER (TERYLENE, DACRON)

Three-quarters the strength of nylon
(but equally strong wet or dry),
polyester does not stretch half as
much, and pre-stretching during
manufacture can remove most of the
latent elasticity it does possess.
Consequently it is recommended for
standing rigging, sheets and halyards,
where stretch is unwanted but high
tensile strength is required, even
replacing wire. It resists acids (and
alkalis, to a lesser extent), oils and
organic solvents. Like nylon, it does
not float and it has about the same
melting point and resistance to
sunlight – but polyester wears better.

POLYETHYLENE (POLYTHENE)

Cheap, light (but it barely floats in
water), without much stretch,

polyethylene is fairly hard-wearing
and durable but has the lowest melting
point of the four "poly" materials. It
is sold in hardware stores as balls of
twine and is used in the fishing
industry, but it is too stiff and
springy for most knot tying.

POLYPROPYLENE

In terms of cost and performance,
this cordage may be ranked between
vegetable fibre and the superior
(nylon, terylene) manmade fibre
cordage. Made from multifilament,
monofilament, staple fibre or split
film, it is the most versatile of
synthetic fibres. Large quantities are
manufactured and sold, at
reasonable prices, via hardware and
DIY shops and stores for all kinds of
mundane work entailing no high
performance risks. It has one-third to
half the breaking strength of nylon
and a much lower melting point –
around 150ºC (302ºF) – rendering it
useless for any task where friction
generates anything approaching that
amount of heat, but, as it is the
lightest of the synthetics, and floats
indefinitely, it is the obvious choice
for lifelines and water-skiing
towlines. It is completely rot-proof
and resistant to most acids, alkalis
and oils, but affected adversely by
bleaching agents and some industrial
solvents, while some cheaper brands
denature in bright sun. For lovers of
traditional cordage, there is a light
brown rope – reliable, hardwearing
and inexpensive – made from
polypropylene to resemble hemp.

Types of Rope

Vegetable fibres are short and must be spun and twisted to create the long yarns and strands needed for rope. It is the countless fibre ends that give traditional ropes their characteristic hairy appearance and useful surface grip. Long synthetic filaments run the full length of the ropes they form, so manmade cordage is smooth – unless the filaments are purposely chopped into shorter lengths of staple fibres to make ropes that recapture the desirable handling qualities of the older natural cordage. More fibres and yarns make thicker cordage, and a rope that is twice the diameter of another will, as a general rule, be four times as strong (because the cross-sectional area has been quadrupled).

LAID

It is the twist and counter-twist imparted during manufacture that holds rope strands together and gives them their geometry, strength and flexibility. If very little tension is applied during the ropemaking process, the product will be floppy and flexible (soft laid), whereas great tension produces stiff (hard laid) stuff. Hard laid lines wear better but soft laid ones are preferable for tying knots. A three-strand rope is known as a hawser (and so is hawser-laid). Three hawsers laid up lefthanded make a nine-strand cable. Four-strand (shroud-laid) rope is less common and requires a core of yarns to fill the hollow space that inevitably occurs at the heart of such ropes. Lefthanded hawsers (and righthanded cables) are rare but not unknown. Textile workers, weavers and braiders prefer the terms S-laid (lefthanded) and Z-laid (righthanded) for the alternating twist and countertwist of yarns, strands and ropes.

BRAIDED

Braided vegetable fibre cordage has always been rare, except in small sizes for flag halyards and sash window cord. In synthetics it is commonplace and in many ways preferable to strands. An 8- or 16-plait (braid) is more flexible and stretches less than laid line. It does not kink, nor does it impart a spinning motion when loaded (as laid lines tend to do). Some braided cordage is hollow. In most, however, a separate core provides strength, elasticity and other essential properties, reinforced by the sheath, which adds extra surface characteristics, such as friction, feel, resistance to abrasion, sunlight and chemicals. This core may take several different forms, in which a braided outer sheath encloses heart strands that can be braided, laid or composed of parallel multifilaments, monofilaments or yarns. Braid-on-braid is acknowledged to be the strongest of cordage constructions and braided synthetic lines are the most versatile of all cordage.

1   2   3   4   5   6   7   8   9

PLAITED

Eight or sixteen ropes, usually nylon, are woven in pairs to create mighty mooring warps for supertankers.

SHEATH-AND-CORE

Climbing ropes are a special class of cordage, often referred to by the European designation kernmantel (core-sheath). Static ropes take the full weight of climbers and are designed for the wear, tear and occasional short fall of regular climbing; while dynamic ropes are used for safety, generally unloaded, but with the extra elasticity and integral strength to cope with potentially disastrous falls and uncontrolled spins. Single ropes are manufactured in 11 mm/^{2}/$_5$ in diameters, plus or minus 5 mm/ ^{1}/$_4$ in, while half-ropes of 9 mm/ ^{3}/$_8$ in diameter, plus or minus 2 mm/^{1}/$_{12}$ in, are intended to be used doubled. Climbing ropes should have high melting points

to absorb the heat generated by abseiling (rappelling) and belaying. Obtain specialist advice on the detailed properties of these ropes and look for the UIAA (Union Internationale des Associations d'Alpinisme) label of approval.

Kernmantel accessory cord, used for slings and other attachments, can be obtained in diameters that range from 4–11 mm/^{1}/$_6$–^{2}/$_5$ in.

Woven nylon webbing comes in widths from 10–75 mm/^{5}/$_{12}$–3 in, but the width most commonly seen is 25 mm/1 in. A tubular tape, resembling a flattened hollow tube, handles and knots easily due to its suppleness, but a flat weave, similar to that found in car seat belts, is stronger, stiffer and has better resistance to wear and abrasion. It is highly versatile and not too expensive for harnesses, belts and slings, and it also makes excellent luggage rack lashings (straps) for cars and vans.

	KEY TO TYPES OF ROPE
1	8-strand nylon, 16 mm/^{2}/$_3$ in anchor braid.
2	3-strand nylon, 14 mm/^{7}/$_{12}$ in hawser.
3	3-strand polyester, 14 mm/^{7}/$_{12}$ in hawser.
4	3-strand spun polyester, 14 mm/^{7}/$_{12}$ in hawser (resembling natural fibre rope).
5	3-strand monofilament polypropylene, 14 mm/^{7}/$_{12}$ in hawser.
6	3-strand staple/spun polypropylene, 14 mm/^{7}/$_{12}$ in hawser.
7	16-plait matt polyester, 14 mm/^{7}/$_{12}$ inbraid-on-braid rope, with an unusual core (itself a16-plait enclosing an 8-plait), creating three concentric layers.
8	16-plait matt polyester, 16 mm/^{2}/$_3$ in braid-on-braid rope (with a double layered core, as above).
9	16-plait pre-stretched polyester, 16 mm/^{2}/$_3$ in braid-on-braid (with an 8-plait core) rope.
10	16-plait Dyneema, 12 mm/^{1}/$_2$ in braid-on-braid rope (with a two-layered core).
11	16-plait Dyneema, 10 mm/ ^{5}/$_{12}$ in braid-on-braid rope (with a two-layered core).
12	16-plait polypropylene, 9 mm/ ^{3}/$_8$ in braid-on-braid cord (with a hard-laid 8-plaid cord core).
13	16-plait polyester, 6 mm/^{1}/$_4$ in sheath-and-core cord (with a heart of four 3-strand strings).
14	8-plait matt polyester, 10 mm/ ^{5}/$_{12}$ in braid-on-braid rope (with an 8-plait core).
15	8-plait multifilament polypropylene, 8 mm/^{1}/$_3$ in braid-on-braid cord (with an 8-plait core).
16	8-plait pre-stretched polyester, 6 mm/^{1}/$_4$ in sheath-and-core cord (with a heart of three 3-strand strings).

10   11   12   13   14   15   16

Breaking Strengths

Ropemakers' brochures and leaflets usually contain tables listing the minimum average breaking load of every type and size of their cordage products. Unfortunately, the data differs from company to company, depending upon the tests and equipment each firm uses, making comparisons difficult.

SPECIFICATIONS

Product specifications may blur the facts: for example, a "mooring line", made for specialized markets, may consist of an elastic nylon core inside a hard-wearing polyester sheath, while many mass-produced and comparatively cheap cordage items, sold for the domestic market, can be much weaker. Nevertheless, an appreciation of the main rope and cordage species can be gained from the following outline. The minimum breaking strength of a 4 mm/⅙ in diameter slim nylon cord of 3-strand or 8-plait construction is likely to be around 320 kg/705 lb, which might withstand two 159-kg/25-stone Japanese sumo wrestlers having a tug-of-war. For standard 3-strand polyester of the same diameter the figure is a trifle lower – 295 kg/650 lb – but an 8-plait construction combined with pre-stretch treatment changes that to around 450 kg/990 lb. Polypropylene of the same diameter is variously quoted at 140 kg/309 lb, 250 kg/551 lb and even 430 kg/925 lb; polyethylene is about 185 kg/408 lb, while the average breaking strength of a 4 mm/⅙ in cord of Dyneema/Admiral 2000/Spectra is a remarkable 650 kg/1,432 lb. To achieve these kinds of performance with natural fibres, it would be necessary to have at least a 25 per cent increase in diameter to 5 mm/⅕ in manila or 33.3 per cent to 6 mm/¼ in sisal.

LARGER SIZES

With a 10 mm/5/12 in thin nylon 3-strand hawser, the minimum breaking strength increases to around 2,400 kg/5,292 lb. That is almost two-and-a-half metric tonnes, the weight of a large motor vehicle. Again, the average figure is somewhat less for polyester at 2,120 kg/about 2 tons; 1,382 kg/1⅓ tons for polypropylene; and 1,090 kg/just over a ton for polyethelene. Dyneema/Admiral 2000/Spectra, by contrast, would be about 4,000 kg/about 4 tons. The same size of rope in manila could only cope with 710 kg/1,565 lb and sisal with 635 kg/1,400 lb.

Finally, for a sizeable 24 mm/1 in rope diameter, the average quoted breaking strengths are: nylon = 13 tonnes/12.8 tons; polyester = 10 tonnes/9.8 tons; polypropylene = 8 tonnes/7.9 tons; polyethylene = 6 tonnes/5.9 tons; and Dyneema/Admiral 2000/Spectra = a stupendous 20 tonnes/19.7 tons. Even the best manila would have to be nearly twice that size (and four times as strong) to match those figures.

✦ LEFT

Vegetable fibre cordage is much weaker and generally has a shorter life than synthetic products.

Synthetic cordage is much stronger and generally has a longer life than products made from vegetable fibre.

COMPARING AND CONTRASTING NATURAL FIBRE AND SYNTHETIC FIBRE ROPES

	NATURAL FIBRES				SYNTHETIC FIBRES			
	Sisal	Cotton	Hemp	Manilla	Polyethylene	Polypropylene	Polyester	Polyamide
Shock loading	●	●	●●●	●●	●	●●●	●●	●●●●
Handling	●	●●●●	●●●	●●	●●●	●●●	●●●●	●●●●
Durability	●	●●	●●●●	●●●	●●	●●●	●●●●	●●●●
Rot & mildew resistance	●	●	●	●	●●●●	●●●●	●●●●	●●●
U.V. resistance	●●●●	●●●●	●●●●	●●●●	●●	●	●●●●	●●
Acid resistance	●	●	●	●	●●●●	●●●●	●●●●	●●●
Alkali resistance	●●	●●	●●	●●	●●●●	●●●●	●●●●	●●●●
Abrasion resistance	●●	●●	●●●	●●●	●●	●●	●●●●	●●●●
Storage	dry	dry	dry	dry	wet or dry	wet or dry	wet or dry	wet or dry
Buoyancy	sinks	sinks	sinks	sinks	floats (just)	floats	sinks	sinks
Melting point*	not affected	not affected	not affected	not affected	about 128°C (about 262°F)	about 150°C (about 302°F)	about 245°C (about 473°F)	about 250°C (about 482°F)

Key: ● poor ●● acceptable ●●● good ●●●● excellent
* Note that cordage softens and weakens at perhaps 20–30 per cent lower temperatures.

SUMMARY

These data take no account of fair wear and tear (including knots), damage or misuse (e.g. shock loading, or excessive friction). Consequently a safe working load will be considerably less – perhaps a fifth to a seventh of the quoted strengths. Then again, it is often necessary to buy synthetic cordage many times stronger than actually required; for example, a 4 mm/⅙ in cord would not match a block and tackle made for 25 mm/1 in rope even though it might be able to cope with the intended load, nor could it be comfortably grasped in the hand and heaved.

Knot tyers do not normally need to know either the molecular structure of cordage or its test data interpreted in charts and graphs. Cavers and climbers, flyers (of gliders and microlight aircraft), and all who calculatingly engage in potentially hazardous pursuits – from astronautics to undersea exploration – can obtain these technical details from the manufacturers. For the average user, a general knowledge of the main types of cordage is all that is needed to buy shrewdly and sensibly.

Care of Cordage

Do not leave rope or smaller stuff (cotton, thread or string) exposed needlessly to bright sunlight. Avoid any chemical contamination (for example, car battery acid). Protect synthetics from heat-generating friction, spark-spitting camp-fires or acetylene-cutting torches, and all other kinds of combustion. Try to avoid letting wet rope freeze. Store cordage in a dark, dry and cool place with good air circulation; relative humidity should be 40–60 per cent and the temperature 10–20°C (50–70°F). Wash dirty ropes in warm water to remove abrasive grit from their fibres and then dry them gently; similarly, at the end of a sailing season, soak and rinse in fresh water ropes that have been exposed to salt crystals. Abrasion can result from careless

◆ ABOVE
WRAPPED & REEF KNOTTED COIL
Rope and smaller cordage alike may be transported this way, in a bag or the boot (trunk) of a motor vehicle, with a realistic hope that it may be retrieved tangle-free at the end of the journey.

◆ LEFT
ALPINE COIL
Climbers favour this means of carrying their ropes.

handling in a rough environment or from ill-fitting blocks, cleats, or fairleads, but fair wear and tear is inevitable, whether it is from regular use or from being kept in the same position for prolonged periods. Even unused rope that has been carefully stored will age and become less reliable.

INSPECTING ROPES

Inspect ropes periodically, metre by metre/yard by yard in a good light, for loose, worn and broken surface yarns and cut strands. Some surface fluffing is inevitable; it is fairly harmless and might actually afford slight protection from further wear. Chemical attack can show as staining and

◆ BELOW
FIGURE-OF-EIGHT COIL
Storekeepers prefer this method, which
provides a loop for hanging ropes.

◆ BELOW
FIREMAN'S COIL
Elegantly simple, this method deserves to
be better known.

used with lifting tackle must be
pensioned off long before they
reach such senescence. Each rope
should have its own log book in
which its working history is
recorded. Communal club ropes
(that anyone might use at any
time) should be retired after two
or three years, but individually
owned and maintained ropes may
be used for four to five years,
then down-graded for teaching
knots and other points of general
use that do not involve climbing.

It has been observed that rope
with a mind of its own, awkward
to manipulate and a trifle
disobedient, is generally at the
height of its powers. By contrast,
rope that is soft and amenable, a
pleasure to handle, should be
condemned and discarded. There
is some truth in this. Do not tread
on rope, allow it to be nipped or
become kinked, or drop it from a
height. Coil ropes loosely and
then hang them up on pegs well
above the floor.

softening. Heat damage is harder
to identify, unless fusing and
glazing are detectable. Internal
wear and damage can be seen by
carefully opening laid strands but
may be concealed in braided stuff
(when the core could be weakened
while the sheath remains relatively
unworn and lacks obvious
damage).

So a risk assessment for braided
lines must also take into account
their recent history of use and
abuse. Worn-out rope looks its
age. It is often attenuated
(weakened by stretching), with a
reduced diameter and a more
acute angle of lay between the
strands. Sheath-and-core ropes
can develop creep, the sheath
moving separately from the heart
strands. Climbing ropes and those

Tools

Acquire a sharp and robust craft knife to cut rope and cord; scissors work only on thin strings and twines. Most of the knots in this book can be tied and tightened with just the fingers, aided now and then with a prod from the pointed cap of a ballpoint pen. A few (such as the Turk's heads) are more easily completed with one or more of the following tools.

GRIPFIDS

Handmade by rope craftsman Stuart Grainger, these resemble small Swedish fids, with the refinement that the tip clings to working strands, pulling them through knotwork as the tool is withdrawn. Two sizes cope with cordage up to either 7 mm/³⁄₁₀ in or 12 mm/½ in diameter.

NETTING NEEDLES

These serve as bobbins for storing quantities of small cords tangle-free and ready for immediate use. Sizes range from a tiny 11.5 cm/ 4½ in to jumbo-sized ones 30 cm/ 12 in or more in length. Shun crudely made ones in favour of those that are polished to a smooth finish. The seller will show you how to load them.

ROUND-BILLED PLIERS

Handy for tightening knots with lots of crossing points. Most high street hardware shops or do-it-yourself superstores will have them. Choose a pair to suit the scale of work: a small size (sometimes called "jeweller's

pliers") will have an overall length of about 10 cm/4 in, with more robust sizes from about 15 cm/6 in upwards.

SWEDISH FIDS*

These are used to poke and prize open gaps through which working strands can be tucked and pulled. Obtainable from yacht chandlers and serious rope stockists, they range in length from about 15 cm/6 in to 38 cm/ 15 in or more. Choose a size to match the scale of your work.

WIRE LOOPS

Homemade from stiff and springy wire 0.25 cm/¹⁄₁₀ in diameter – or thinner – inserted securely into a handle, these are indispensable alternatives to fids when working with smaller stuff.

♦ BELOW
Tying elaborate knots is made easier with one or more handy tools (see key to illustration).

KEY TO TOOLS	
1	Netting needle (large)
2	Netting needle (medium)
3	Netting needle (small)
4	Gripfid (large)
5	Gripfid (small)
6	Hollow "Swedish" fid (small)
7	Hollow "Swedish" fid (large)
8	Homemade wire loop (large)
9	Homemade wire loop (small)
10	Homemade wire loop (medium)
11	Jeweller's pliers
12	Round-billed pliers

* Originally fids were solid hardwood spikes. They can occasionally be found in antique shops or markets as collectable treen (lathe-turned wood).

Cutting & Securing Ends

TYING & TAPING

Before cutting any natural fibre cordage, first tape or tie it to prevent fraying. Adhesive tape is the least attractive option – and unacceptable on finished craftwork – but it is used a lot in preparatory stages as an easy alternative to whipping. Wrap where the cut is to be made and then simply slice the tape in half to achieve two bound ends at a stroke. Alternatively, tie a pair of strangle or constrictor knots, one on either side of where the cut is to be made.

HEATING & SEALING

This is now widely practised by ropeworkers and riggers. There is no need to tape or tie heat-sealed ends. Rope manufacturers and stockists have electrically heated guillotines to cut-and-seal the ropes and cords they sell. These cost too much for most of us, so the comparatively cool yellow flame of a struck match may have to do on small stuff. For large diameters, or to cut-and-seal a batch of strands, heat the blade of an old penknife in the blue flame of a blow-torch until the tip and edge glow cherry-red. Pause to re-heat it every few seconds for a clean and fast cut. Nylon melts, drips and burns with whitish smoke and a smell said to resemble fish or celery; it may even flash into a small flame (easily blown out). Polyester melts, drips and burns with dense black smoke and a smell like mushrooms. Polypropylene and

TYING

1 Tie two constrictor knots, one either side of where the cut will be made.

TAPING

1 Wrap a turn or two of adhesive tape around the rope or cord.

HEAT SEALING 1

With an electric guillotine or a heated knife blade (not shown), cordage and small diameter ropes may be neatly cut and sealed.

2 Slice vertically down halfway between the two binding knots already tied.

2 Cut vertically down through the middle of the taped portion.

HEAT SEALING 2

Use the naked flame of a match or cigarette lighter for a quick but often lumpy seal.

polyethylene react at lower temperatures, shrinking rapidly away from the source of heat. It is possible to pinch the soft heated ends to a point, rolling them between forefinger and thumb, before they harden, but take care

to wet the fingertips first or it may cause a burn and blister. A cord that appears to be synthetic but actually chars and even ignites without melting, is probably made from rayon, which comes from wood pulp.

Terms & Techniques

Anyone who ties a knot is described in knotting circles as a tyer (not tier) since the former is unambiguous while the latter has a different meaning when written.

SIMPLE TERMS

The end actively involved in the tying process is referred to as the **working end** or sometimes – by anglers – as the **tag end**; the inactive remainder is known as the **standing part** and **standing end**. Doubling a line so that two parts are brought close together creates a **bight**. If this is done to locate the exact centre of the bit of stuff in hand, then one is said to **middle** it. Once the two adjacent parts cross, a bight turns into a loop; a further twist creates a couple of **elbows**, while the process of turning a bight or loop into an improvised eye by wrapping the end several times around the standing part is referred to as **dogging**. Any loop that is pulled

> ### NOTE
>
> Several categories of knots in this book have been illustrated in thicker cordage than would ordinarily be used to tie them. For instance, the whippings and fishermen's knots would actually be tied in very fine twines and monofilaments. This has been done to make the tying process clearer. The characteristically barrel-shaped knots for use in angling monofilaments do not always tighten as easily in larger cordage – but they can, with a little more time and care, be shaped and tightened to make useful general purpose holdfasts.

so small that it deforms and damages a rope becomes a **kink**.

The word **rope** is generally defined as meaning any plaited, braided or laid (in strands) product over 10 mm ($5/12$ in) in diameter, although there are exceptions (for example, some

climbing ropes are 9 mm/$3/8$ in diameter). Anything much smaller is referred to as **cord**, **string**, **twine** or **thread**. Rope and cord are collectively called **cordage** but, more commonly, **stuff**. A rope or cord dedicated to a particular job becomes a **line** (tow line, washing line, lifeline, throwing or heaving line), or acquires an even more specific label (lanyard, lashing or lassoo). A lightweight throwing or heaving line that is used to haul a heavier line across an intervening space is known as a **messenger**. The terms **plait** and **braid** are virtually interchangeable. There are, however, some who say that braids are flat while plaits have a three-dimensional cross-section.

Ropeworkers often "take a **turn**" in order to check a load by means of the friction it applies. Wrapping the working end an extra amount to bring it alongside the standing part, so as to tie it off, produces a **round turn**. Converting a single-ply knot to two, three (or more) ply involves following the original **lead** of the knot around with the working end. The place within a knot where the collective friction of its parts is concentrated is known as the **nip**. The tuck that finally secures a knot, preventing it from collapsing or unravelling, is the **locking tuck**. A simple loop is an **overhand loop** when the working end lies on top of the standing part, becoming an **underhand loop** if the working end goes beneath the standing part.

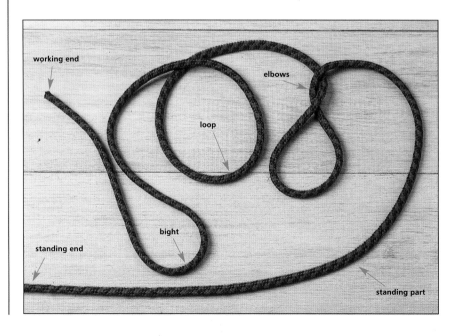

working end

elbows

loop

bight

standing end

standing part

1 More often than not, a clove hitch may have been tied with the working end.

2 But slide the knot sideways off its foundation – and it will fall apart.

3 Once separated from its foundation, nothing remains of the knot but the line in which it was tied.

4 To re-tie the clove hitch, this time in the bight, first cast an overhand loop.

5 Create a second underhand loop immediately alongside the first one.

6 Twist the loops to overlap them. The resulting clove hitch may be slid back on to its foundation.

TYING TECHNIQUES

Most knots can be tied in more than one way. The methods illustrated have been chosen either because they are easier to learn or to photograph clearly. Practised knot tyers develop more dextrous ways to tie knots that are almost sleight of hand. Discover these slicker and quicker tying tricks for yourself: with a completed knot in your hands, back-track, untying the knot a step at a time, to see how it is created. A short cut may occur to you. Re-tie it that way in future.

Tying a knot "in the bight" means doing so without using the working end. When a hitch or a binding knot collapses to nothing if slid from the foundation around which it was tied or a loop knot can be unravelled without recourse to its ends (in other words, it "unties in the bight"), then it can be tied in the bight. This is the "law of hitch & bight" proposed by Harry Asher in the mid-1980s. A surprising number of knots may be tied this way. Knowing the principle can also enable knot tyers to spot subtle differences in seemingly identical knots: for example, the bag knot can be tied in the bight but the miller's knot cannot.

Most knots must be drawn up gradually so as to remove slack and daylight before gently pulling on each end and standing part in turn to create a knot that remains snug and firm.

BASIC KNOTS, BENDS & HITCHES

"Every knot is an exercise in friction ... extreme simplicity can only be had at the expense of effectiveness."

(BRION TOSS –
THE RIGGER'S APPRENTICE, 1984)

All knotting may be summed up under three main headings: Knots, Bends and Hitches. A hitch attaches a line to a post, rail, spar, ring or even another rope; a bend joins two ropes together; a knot is anything other than a bend or a hitch (including stopper knots, binding knots and loop knots) although the word "knot" is also used, sometimes confusingly, in a general way to refer even to bends and hitches. Discover how easily you can tie these 20 basic knots. All you will need is two lengths of flexible cord, each 1–2 m/3–6½ ft long and from 5–10 mm/ ⅕–⁵⁄₁₂ in in diameter.

Most cordage will fray unless the ends are securely treated in some way. A better-looking treatment than taping, tying and heat sealing is a whipping of some kind, and four whipped ends are detailed in this section.

Simple, Overhand or Thumb Knot

This is the most elementary stopper knot, to prevent small stuff (cotton, thread or string) from fraying or pulling out of a hole through which it has been threaded. Its uses range from securing thread in a needle to tying loose change into the corner of a handkerchief when on the beach or anywhere else where deep pockets are temporarily not available. Nobody ever has to be taught to tie this knot. It just comes naturally.

1 Make an overhand loop in the small stuff that is to be tied.

2 Tuck the working end through the loop already formed and pull on the standing end to tighten the knot.

Overhand Knot with Drawloop

Drawloops act as quick releases, and may also strengthen some knots by bulking them up with an extra knot part. Overlooked and underrated by many knot tyers, drawloops deserve to be used more, and will from time to time be recommended in this book.

Start to tie a simple overhand knot but stop before the working end has been fully pulled through.

Two Strand Overhand Knot

This is another knot that the youngest person can tie instinctively. It creates a bigger stopper knot, for cottons or domestic string, and also acts to hold cords together as long as they lie in the same direction, for example, to prevent a waist tie in pyjamas, swimming trunks or tracksuit trousers (sweatpants) from pulling out when not in use. NB: This is not a bend because the two cords are not aligned to be pulled in opposite directions.

1 Place the two strings or cords to be tied parallel and together.

2 Tie a simple overhand knot. Tighten, taking care to keep the lines parallel (like railway tracks) throughout.

Double Overhand Knot

This forms a chunkier stopper knot than the simple overhand knot, although it will not block a larger hole. It is, however, an indispensable technique for other knots that are based upon it.

1 Tie an overhand knot – but tuck the working end a second time.

2 Gently pull both ends apart, at the same time twisting them in opposite directions. In the example shown, the lefthand thumb goes up and away from the tyer, the righthand thumb down and away. The cord dictates what it wants to do; simply go along with it. See how a diagonal knot part wraps itself around – let it happen. Pull on both ends at the same time to tighten this knot.

Triple (and Multiple) Overhand Knots

Three (or more) initial tucks produce triple or multiple overhand knots. These can make shortenings and embellishments, such as those seen in the ropes around the waists of nuns and monks, who used this triple knot as a symbolic reference to their threefold sacred vows.

2 Pull both ends, rotating them in different directions so that a diagonal wrapping turn appears.

1 Tie a double overhand knot, then tuck the working end a third time.

3 Shape the emerging knot to bed all of the knot parts down snugly. Tighten by pulling both ends apart.

Strangle Knot

A double overhand knot, tied around something, makes a strangle knot. Use it to seize cut ends of cordage and prevent them from fraying; to secure rolls of anything from carpets to technical drawings and wallpaper, or to clamp do-it-yourself and hobbyists' bits-and-pieces together while the glue hardens. Several other useful binding knots are featured in this book; but, for a start, this one is as good as any. Try it also with a drawloop.

1 Produce a double overhand knot but at this stage keep it very loose.

2 Insert whatever is to be bound, ensure the overriding diagonal lies between the other two knot parts, and tighten the knot by pulling on both ends. The ends can then be cut off short.

Single Hitch

Commonly referred to as a half hitch, alone this is an unreliable means of attachment except for the most temporary and trivial of purposes (when a drawloop might help) but it is the means of finishing off other more substantial working hitches.

1 Tie the ubiquitous overhand knot around something firm, such as a fat felt tip pen, to discover how this careful rearrangement traps the working end.

2 Leave a longer working end, which is not completely pulled through, for a drawloop.

Two Half Hitches

Two half hitches are the tried and trusted way to secure a line to a ring, rail or anything. They are always identical, i.e. the working end goes the same way around the standing part in both cases.

1 Tie a single half hitch with the working end of the line.

2 Add an identical second half hitch and draw them snugly together to complete this useful attachment.

33

Round Turn & Two Half Hitches

This is a classic hitch, comparatively strong and secure, the name of which describes it exactly. It can be used to secure a boat, to tow a broken-down vehicle or secure a load.

1 Take a turn around the anchorage, bring the working end alongside the standing part, and apply a half hitch.

2 Add an identical half hitch to complete this dependable knot.

Overhand Knot & Half Hitch

This loop knot has been used by weavers to rig looms, by Inuits (Eskimos) to string bows, by anglers as a leader loop for tackle, and for starting to tie parcels. It is sometimes called a packer's knot.

1 Tie an overhand knot with a large drawloop and adjust the loop to the required size.

2 Wrap and tuck a half hitch with the working end around the standing part. Tighten by pulling on each one of the loop legs in turn.

Overhand Loop

Use this very basic knot in thin stuff for starting parcels and other lashings. It does not easily untie and is therefore a knot that must generally be cut off and discarded after use.

1 Double one end of a cord (make a bight) and form a loop in the doubled end.

2 Tie an overhand knot, taking the trouble to keep the knot parts neatly parallel throughout the knot. Tighten by pulling on each one of the four knot parts in turn.

Double Overhand Loop

This loop is bulkier and slightly stronger than the previous one.

Do not attempt to untie it – cut it off after use.

1 With a somewhat longer bight, tie a double overhand knot.

2 Uncross any twisted knot parts and remove any slack until the knot assumes its characteristic shape. Then tighten gradually, pulling on each of the four knot parts in turn.

Surgeon's Loop

This is a triple overhand loop, stronger for the extra tuck, and is recommended for angling lines.

Make this knot in dispensable stuff as it is easier to cut it off than to untie it.

1 Make a fairly long bight and tie a treble overhand knot in it.

2 Eliminate any unevenness and mould it with your fingers into a smooth barrel-shaped knot. Anglers may spit on monofilaments to lubricate them.

Simple Noose

This simplest of running (sliding) loops is useful to start parcels or other lashings.

Working away from the short end, tie an overhand knot (with drawloop) in what would normally be regarded as the standing part of the line, and pull it tight.

Scaffold Knot

This is a strong, secure sliding loop. Use it when an eye must be protected from chafe by means of a metal or plastic liner (called a "thimble"). Tighten the loop to grip and hold this particular bit of hardware. With practised fingers, this knot can be tied in no more than 30 seconds and the beauty of it is that the more the strain that's put on it, the tighter this knot will grip.

1 Make a bight and tie a double overhand knot with the working end around the standing part of the line.

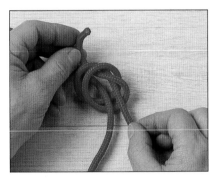

2 Pull the end and the appropriate leg of the loop in opposite directions to tighten the knot.

Multiple Scaffold Knot

A triple overhand knot will make a double scaffold knot, which is perhaps slightly stronger. A multiple knot results from a multiple overhand knot, but there is probably little benefit from doing this other than to produce a handsomely handy bulk.

1 Tie a straight forward triple overhand knot in the working end around the standing part.

2 Pull the end and the appropriate loop leg in opposite directions to tighten the knot.

Overhand Bend

Also known as the tape knot, this knot is recommended for the flat or tubular woven webbing (tape) used by cavers and climbers – although it works in anything from the largest cables to the finest angling monofilaments.

1 Tie an overhand knot in the end of one of the two lines to be joined. Insert the end of the second line.

2 Follow the lead of the original knot with the second working end.

3 For a twofold knot, ensure that all knot parts are parallel and that the short ends emerge at the top of the knot as there is some evidence that it may be stronger this way. Pull the standing parts to tighten.

Fisherman's Knot

The reliable fisherman's knot can be used for anything and everything from domestic to heavy industrial tasks. This is a knot that can be untied if it has been made from rope, but if you make it out of string you will have to cut it off.

1 Lay the two lines parallel and close to one another, tying an overhand knot with one end around the standing part of the other.

2 Turn the half-completed knot end-for-end and tie an identical overhand knot with the other end. Pull first on both working ends to tighten the individual knots, then on the standing parts to unite and tighten the knot.

Double Fisherman's Knot

The stronger double fisherman's knot is known to anglers as a grinner knot (presumably because of the gaping mouth formed before the knots slide shut). It is a reasonably secure knot.

1 Place the two lines parallel and close together, tying a double overhand knot with one working end around the other standing part.

2 Turn the half-completed knot end-for-end and tie a second double overhand knot with the other end. Tighten individual knots before pulling on the standing parts to close the knot.

Triple Fisherman's Knot

A triple fisherman's knot is an angler's double grinner knot and is used for thinner, springier or more slippery lines.

Proceed as for a double fisherman's knot – but use triple overhand knots – and tighten similarly.

Strength & Security

Knots weaken the rope, cord or string in which they are tied. An unwanted overhand knot allowed to remain in a fishing line or washing line, for instance, will more than halve the breaking strength. Bulky knots are better, the double fisherman's or grinner knot preserving 65 to 70 per cent of the cordage strength and the blood knot 85 to 90 per cent; while the bimini twist is claimed by some to be 100 per cent efficient (in other words, as strong as the unknotted line). Climbers, whose lives literally hang upon their knots; anglers, keen to preserve expensive tackle and to catch that record-breaking fish; ropeworking assault, rescue or survey teams; lifting tackle operatives on construction sites – all choose and use strong knots.

Security is a different consideration. A strong knot that slips and slides, spills, capsizes or otherwise comes undone, is less secure than one that holds firm. Some knots are secure enough when carefully assembled and placed under a steady load but loosen and come adrift if intermittently jerked or repeatedly shaken.

Since strength and security are different characteristics, knots that combine both of them would seem to be ideal – why bother with any others? This is because ease of tying and untying are often essential. Simplicity too may be desirable. So, when they can get away with it, knot tyers knowingly trade off one quality

against the other. Indeed some classic knots, despite long established reputations for reliability, are surprisingly weak and insecure when put to the test. The common bowline is barely 45 per cent strong and in stiff or slick rope can easily be made to spill.

◆ ABOVE
Strengthened bowline secured with an overhand knot.

Knots can be made more secure. For example, the relatively strong figure-of-eight loop may be made more secure by attaching the short end of the rope to its adjacent standing part with a double overhand knot (*above left*). Similarly, the common bowline may be both strengthened and made more secure with the extra turn of this double (or climber's) version, the working end of which is further safeguarded with an overhand knot to the nearest leg of the loop (*left*). The reef knot is essentially weak, but the two ends may be secured with a couple of double overhand knots (*above centre*). A proprietary brand of chock (*above right*), known as a "wallnut" and used for mountaineering and related activities, is attached to a strop made from outstandingly strong Spectra accessory cord. This is tied with a double fisherman's knot. Security is assured by taping both ends to their adjacent standing parts.

Common Whipping

Comparatively quick to apply, this traditional treatment for a rope's end is also the most likely to come untied.

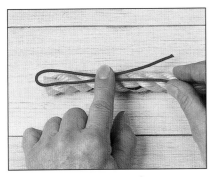

1 Make a long bight and lay it along the rope as shown.

2 Begin to wrap the working end around the rope, trapping both legs of the bight within the initial turn. Wrapping turns are made in the opposite direction to the lay of the rope, so that any tendency for the rope to unlay will tighten the whipping.

3 Continue to wrap tightly towards the rope's end, taking care to keep each turn snugly and neatly against the preceding one. Continue until the whipping is at least as long as the diameter of the rope.

4 *(left)* Tuck the working end through the remaining portion of the bight.

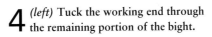

5 *(right)* Pull the working end (not illustrated) to reduce the bight until it traps the working end; then pull harder, so that the working end is dragged beneath the wrapping turns. Stop when the interlocked elbows reach the centre of the whipping. If they saw through and break the twine, either wrap less tightly or use stronger stuff; in any case they make a bulge beneath the wrapping turns. Trim the ends.

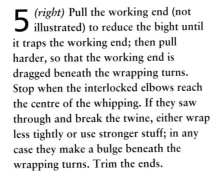

Perfected Whipping

This improved version eliminates the harsh elbows that are a feature of the common whipping.

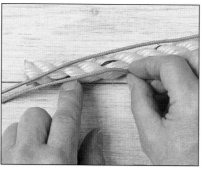

1 Lay both ends of the whipping twine together, pointing in opposite directions, on the rope.

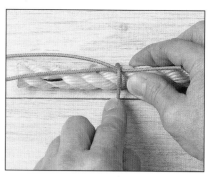

2 Begin to wrap with that part of the twine furthest from the rope's end.

3 Continue to wrap as tightly and neatly as possible, keeping the two underlying twine parts parallel and together, and untangling the working bight (each completed revolution) from the rope's end.

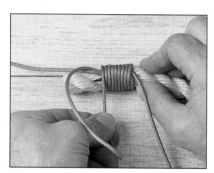

4 As the working bight shrinks, remove the twist that is inevitably imparted to it (better still, with practice, at the start insert a counter-twist that will unwind as the work progresses).

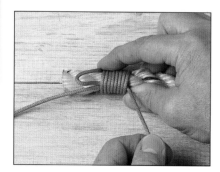

5 Pull on the end of the twine to remove all slack from the final wrapping turn, before pulling steadily on both ends to secure and finish off the whipping.

West Country Whipping

Some dismiss this as ugly and not a proper whipping. It is certainly not as neat as other whippings, but more pragmatic knot tyers point out that it stays put when a common whipping comes undone. In practice, the alternate half knots, with repetition, begin to take on a rugged bumpiness that is not unattractive.

1 Tie an overhand knot about 2.5 cm/ 1 in from the rope's end.

2 Turn the rope face down and tie an identical second overhand knot on the reverse side.

3 Turn the work face up again, and tie a third overhand knot alongside the first one. Repeat this process of simple knotting on alternate sides.

4 Finish off with a reef (square) knot, and poke the ends back beneath the completed whipping with a handy pointed implement.

Sailmaker's Whipping

No matter how well tied, after much wear and tear, whippings do inevitably come loose and come off. For ropes that flog about in the wind, such as flag halyards and running rigging aboard sailing craft, this tough variant is tied into the rope's strands, which gives it extra strength and security. Alternatively, on braided rope, the riding turns that secure it may be stitched right through with a robust needle.

1 Unlay the rope's end for a distance of about 5 cm/2 in and pass a bight of whipping twine over one strand, so that both ends of the twine emerge between the other two strands.

2 Re-lay the strands and select either end of the twine with which to begin the whipping.

3 Wrap neatly and tightly from the bight towards the rope's end.

4 Continue until the length of the whipping at least equals the diameter of the rope.

5 Lay the bight along the rope so that it spirals with one leg following each of the grooves created by the strand it originally enclosed.

6 Loop the bight over the strand and pull it tight with the standing end of the twine.

7 Lay this end of the twine in a similar helix along the remaining third groove.

8 Tie the two ends securely between the strands, preferably with a reef (square) knot. (Note – A granny knot was used here, as it was easier to conceal in the picture of the finished whipping, given the thick cord.)

BENDS

"To bend two Cabells or Roapes together . . .
when we meane to take them a-sunder againe."

(Sir Henry Manwayring –
The Sea-man's Dictionary, 1644)

A bend is any knot that joins two ropes or
other lines together. As a general rule, it should
be possible to untie bends after use, for rope is
a costly item that may be re-used later for
another purpose. Restrict untieable knots to
string, anglers' monofilaments and other such
stuff, from which they can be cut off and
discarded when no longer needed. Most bends
are made in two separate ends of identical
material but some, for example a sheet bend
and the different heaving line bends, are
intended for use when two lines differ
noticeably in diameter or stiffness. The
lightweight binding knots that join the two
ends of the same length of line (for example.
parcel twine or shoe laces) are knots – as
opposed to bends – but in more substantial
stuff bends are employed to create cargo
strops and endless slings for caving
and climbing.

Flemish Bend

Old seamen viewed this bend with disfavour, because it tended to jam in natural fibre ropes, but it suits synthetic cordage. Climbers like it because it is easily learned and readily checked by a team leader.

1 Make a loop in one end of one of the two lines to be joined.

2 Impart half a twist, in this instance left thumb going up and away – that is, anticlockwise (counterclockwise).

3 Tuck the working end as shown to create the characteristic figure-of-eight outline.

4 Introduce the second line, with its working end parallel to and alongside the first one.

5 Follow the lead of the first rope with the second, keeping to the outside of the first bend (evidence suggests that this makes a stronger knot).

6 Continue around and through the original knot, transferring to the inside of the second bend.

7 Complete the two-ply knot, then tighten it a bit at a time by pulling on each working end and standing part in turn.

Double Figure-of-Eight Bend

This knot is similar in function to the fisherman's knot but, unlike that knot, it is bilaterally symmetrical (both sides look the same). Several knots with a figure-of-eight layout are referred to as Flemish knots, and an alternative name for this one is the Flemish bend. Leave the knots a few inches apart for a knot that will absorb a sudden jerk or snatch by sliding before it holds.

1 Tie a figure-of-eight knot in one of the two lines and insert the second line through the first knot.

2 Then begin to tie another figure-of-eight knot.

3 Complete the second figure-of-eight knot, which, when the work is turned end-for-end, must be identical to the first one.

4 Pull first on the working ends to remove the slack from the individual knots, then on both standing parts to slide them together.

Linfit Knot

Thick and springy materials need an alternative to the double fisherman's (or grinner) knot, and this one was devised by angler Owen K. Nuttall.

1 Make a bight in each of the two lines to be joined and lay them one across the other, as shown.

2 Take the working end of the upper line around the back of the lower bight from right to left.

3 Bring the working end of the lower line across the front, taking it from left to right.

4 Pass the lefthand working end in a clockwise direction around the lefthand standing part.

5 Tuck this lefthand working end from behind and bring it up through the lefthand bight.

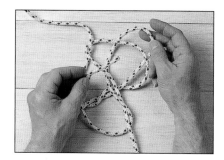

6 Bring the righthand working end anticlockwise (counterclockwise) around the righthand standing part.

7 Tuck this working end from in front down through the righthand bight. Remove the slack from this arrangement until you have a symmetrical form, with both ends emerging at right angles to the standing parts and on the same side of the knot. Pull on each working and standing end in turn to tighten the completed knot.

Zeppelin Bend

This is one of a family of bends comprising two interlocked overhand knots. It is both strong and secure, and the fact that both working ends stick out at right angles to their standing parts is only a minor snag that may be somewhat unsightly but is rarely inconvenient. The American naval officer and aeronautics hero Charles Rosendahl required his massive dirigible Los Angeles to be moored with this bend – and no other – in the 1930s; and the US Navy continued to employ it for lighter-than-air ships until as recently as 1962. Rosendahl's method of tying this knot was more awkward than the one illustrated, which was devised at a later date – sometime in the 1980s – by Ettrick W. Thomson. Use it in anything from heavyweight cables and hawsers to the smallest of cords.

1 Hold the two ropes together, with their ends in the same direction.

2 Form a loop with the working end of the rope that is closest to you.

3 Take the working end around behind both ropes and bring it back through its own loop.

4 Lift the standing part of the other rope towards its working end.

5 Pass the second working end beneath its own standing part and tuck it through the loop that is formed. Pull on both working ends and standing parts to remove any slack to tighten this knot.

Adjustable Bend

Use this bend with the twin knots somewhat separated. Under a moderate and steady load, they will remain apart. If a sudden extra load is exerted upon them, however, they slide and so absorb some of the strain. The knots may be tied in rope or webbing (tape). The Canadian climber Robert Chisnall devised this bend sometime before 1982.

1 Lay the two lengths of cord parallel to each other. Then turn one of the two lines around the other, wrapping towards its nearest end.

2 Take a second turn with the first line around the second one.

3 Pass the working end around and beneath both the wrapped line and its own standing part.

4 Bring the working end back down in front of the second line, tucking it under its own final turn.

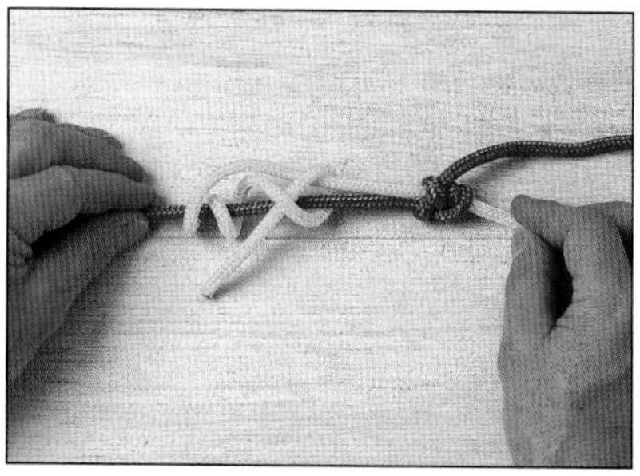

5 Turn the half-completed knot end-for-end and, using the second line, make an identical second knot about 5 cm/2 in from the first one.

Hunter's Bend

This young relative of the zeppelin bend is probably its equal. American Phil D. Smith devised it during the Second World War, and he simply called it a rigger's bend; but English physician Edward Hunter rediscovered it in 1978, and the worldwide publicity he achieved for the knot led to the establishment in 1982 of the International Guild of Knot Tyers. The tying method illustrated is the one Dr Hunter used.

1 Place the two lines to be joined parallel and beside one another.

2 Make twin loops, taking care that the two lines remain parallel.

3 Take the working end from the front of the loops around to the back.

4 Tuck this end from behind through to the front of both loops.

5 Bring the other working end up in front of the two loops.

6 Tuck this end through the loop from front to back, in the opposite direction to the first end.

7 Begin to remove the slack from the knot, taking care that the working ends do not come out of the loops.

8 Pull each working end and standing part, in turn, until the knot is fully tightened.

Surgeon's Knot

Often recommended as a binding knot (perhaps wrongly, as it does yield a certain amount of slack in tightening), this makes a neat and secure bend, even in synthetic cordage. It is possible that it may once have been used in surgical sutures, hence its name. Usually seen in small cordage, it can be a worthwhile knot to use in all types of rope.

1 Cross the working ends of the two ropes to be joined, in this instance left over right.

2 Tie a half knot, noting how the two parts twine lefthanded or anticlockwise (counterclockwise).

3 Take an extra tuck and then bring the working ends together again, this time right over left.

4 Tie a final half knot, of opposite handedness to the first couple, with the two parts twining righthanded (clockwise). To tighten the knot, first hold each working end with its adjacent standing part; but finally just pull on the standing parts, allowing the upper half knot to twist slightly so that it overlays the completed knot diagonally from corner to corner.

Harness Bend

As its name implies, this knot was
known to carters and waggoners
in the days of horse-drawn goods
vehicles because it works equally
well in leather or rawhide strips.
It will also join materials as
diverse as raffia or fence wire.

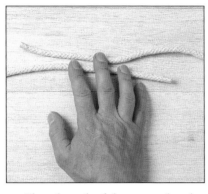

1 Place the ends of the two cords to be
joined parallel to each other and
close together.

2 Keeping the two cords together, take
one working end under and then
over the other standing part.

3 Bring this end around to complete
one end of the knot.

4 Pass the other working end beneath
the nearby standing part.

5 Make a half hitch with this end.
Then pull the arrangement tight, so
that the ends emerge on opposite sides of
the knot.

Double Harness Bend with Parallel Ends

Many knot tyers prefer
symmetrical bends, which are
often better looking and can be
easier to learn, tie and memorize.
This version is also a little
stronger and more secure than
the harness bend.

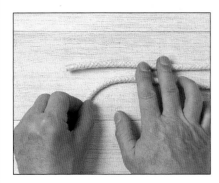

1 Place the two lines to be joined
parallel and together.

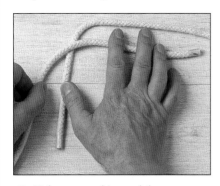

2 Take one working end down
beneath the other standing part.

3 Then bring this end up and back
over the other line.

4 Tuck the end down between
both lines to complete one half
of the knot.

5 Turn the half-completed knot end-
for-end and tie an identical crossing
knot with the other working end. Work
the knot tight, so that both ends protrude
together from the same side of the knot.

Strop Bend

Any two eyes, loops and endless strops or slings may be interlaced this way. It can amuse young children to make long multi-coloured chains of elastic bands with a series of these knots; but the strop bend can also be put to hard labour on construction sites and dockyards.

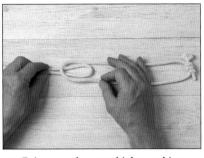

1 Bring together two bights and insert one up through the other.

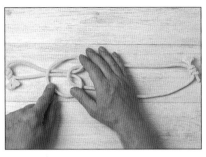

2 Double the working bight of the two back upon itself.

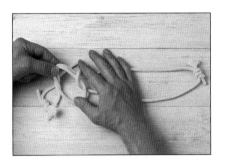

3 Pick up the standing parts of the working loop to draw them through the secondary loop.

4 Pull the remainder of the working loop completely through itself.

5 Begin to pull the two bights in opposite directions, one away from the other.

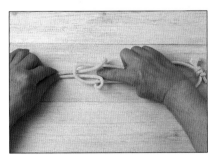

6 Continue until the two bights are snugly interlocked with one another.

7 Tighten by pulling on both pairs of loop legs at once. While this knot resembles a reef (square) knot in layout, the dynamics are very different, and it will, of course, only come undone if one of the lines breaks.

Blood Knot with Inward Coil

This is one of the several classic angling knots that, because of their numerous compact wrapping turns, are collectively known as blood or barrel-shaped knots. Numerous wrapping turns make this knot both strong and secure. It is primarily used by anglers, who tie it in their fine lines, but it can prove equally useful, tied in thicker cordage, out of water.

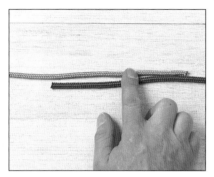

1 Bring two lines, facing in opposite directions, close together, and lay them parallel.

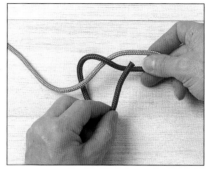

2 With one of the working ends, begin to apply wrapping turns.

3 The first wrap should go around the front and then down the back of both lines.

4 Ensure that the first wrapping turn encloses both of the lines to be joined so as to trap its own standing part.

5 Try to make each wrapping turn lie snugly and tightly beside the previous one.

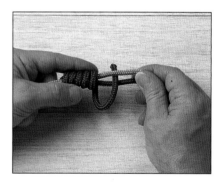

6 Complete five or six turns, then tuck and trap the working end between both lines.

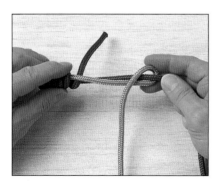

7 With the other working end, begin the wrapping process again.

8 Repeat the previous steps, wrapping in towards the middle of the emerging knot.

9 Finally tuck the second working end down through the centre of the knot (in the opposite direction to the other end). Mould all of the turns tight, from the outside in, and then pull on the two ends to remove any slack.

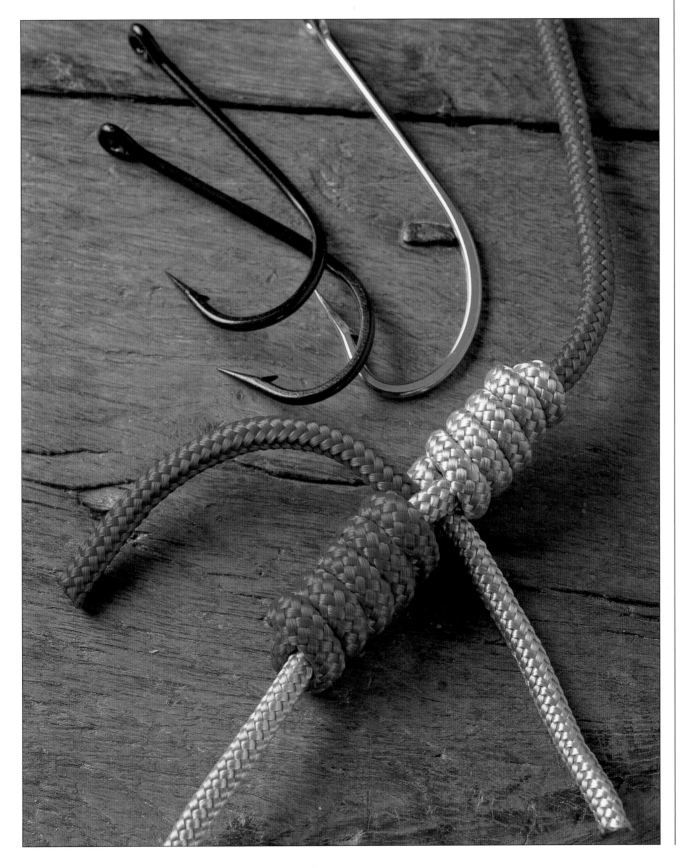

Carrick Bend with Ends Opposed

This knot name dates from the 18th century, but its actual origin is obscure. At Carrick-on-Suir in Ireland, the Elizabethan plasterwork of Ormonde Castle is embellished with numerous carrick bends moulded in relief, while a "carrack" was a type of medieval trading ship, from which perhaps comes Carrick Road outside Falmouth Harbour in Cornwall. Recommended for large hawsers and cables, this bend has acquired a reputation for strength, when it actually reduces the breaking strength of the ropes to about 65 per cent. Nevertheless, given today's strong synthetic cordages, it is still a considerable heavyweight among bends. It is said to be more secure if it is tied in such a way that the working ends emerge on opposite sides of the knot.

1 Make a loop with the working end of one of the two lines to be joined lying (in this instance) over its own standing part.

2 Place the second line over the initial loop, in the direction shown, and pass the working end beneath the other standing part.

3 Begin a second loop, taking the second working end over the first working end.

4 With the second end, make a locking tuck that goes under-over-under to complete the knot. Pull on the two standing parts to tighten the knot, when the flat heraldic outline will capsize into a compact and different form.

Carrick Bend with Ends Adjacent

With the ends on the same side of the knot, the carrick bend becomes the heraldic device once known as the Wake knot, the badge of the Saxon leader Hereward the Wake who in 1071 AD revolted against William the Conqueror. The late Desmond Mandeville, who researched the relationships of bends for more than 25 years, discovered there was one knot to which all were related and to which every family tree he drew returned – this one. Use this knot for decorative purposes, retaining the flat and open layout. It can look most attractive when used as a curtain tie-back, to secure a dressing gown cord, or even on an antique chaise longue.

1 Make a loop with the working end of one of the two lines to be joined going over the standing part.

2 Lay the working end of the second line beneath the initial loop, pointing in the direction shown.

3 Bring the second working end over the other working end.

4 Begin a second loop by taking the second new working end under the other standing part.

5 Make a locking tuck that goes over-under-over to secure the lefthand half of the knot.

6 Unlike the ends opposed version, keep this knot flat and open.

Vice Versa

Some intractable materials – such as wet and slimy leather thongs or bungee (elastic) shock cord – are difficult to keep in place and slither out of other bends. They can, however, be tamed with this relatively new knot from the fertile mind of Harry Asher, first published in 1989. The extra security can only be achieved with the additional tucks and turns that are features of this knot.

1 Lay the two lines to be joined parallel and together.

2 Take the righthand working end and bring it beneath the other standing part.

3 Pass the end over the other line and then tuck it beneath itself.

4 Take the other working end to the left, over the first of the two lines.

5 Bring the second working end back beneath the other line and up past the front of the knot (with no tuck).

6 Cross the righthand end over the lefthand end and tuck it through the lefthand loop alongside its own standing part. Similarly, take hold of what has become the righthand end.

7 Finally, tuck the remaining working end through the righthand loop alongside its own standing part. Gently pull on all four of the emerging lines at once to securely tighten this knot.

Sheet Bend

This knot is neither strong nor secure. It reduces the strength of lines by 55 per cent, and can spill if subject to spasmodic jerking. This said, it is part of every knot tyer's basic repertoire. When it attaches a lanyard to a loop it may be referred to as a becket hitch, and, tied (by a different method) in yarns, it is called the weaver's knot.

1 Create a bight in the end of one of the ropes to be tied.

2 Take the second rope and tuck it up through the bight.

3 Pass the working end beneath the bight.

4 Tuck the working end beneath itself in such a way that both short ends are located on the same side of the completed knot (with many materials, it seems to be more secure this way).

Double Sheet Bend

If the two lines are of dissimilar size or stiffness, make the bight in the bigger or tougher one, and tie this double sheet bend to counteract any tendency for it to straighten and so spill the knot. There is no need for a third tuck. If this knot is insufficient, try the racking bend.

1 Make a bight in the larger of the two ropes to be joined.

2 Take the second of the lines and tuck it up through the bight.

3 Bring the end around and beneath the bight in the other rope.

4 Tuck the working end beneath itself so that both short ends are located on the same side of the knot (with many materials it is more secure this way).

5 Bring the working end around and beneath the bight and its own standing line once again, keeping it to the right of the original pass.

6 Finally, tuck the end through alongside the initial tuck to complete the double knot.

One-Way Sheet Bend

When a sheet bend is likely to be dragged over or through obstructions, the two short ends can be streamlined by means of this adaption. Use this simple but effective modification for ropes that may be towed in water, passed through a rocky crevice or even exposed to gale-force winds. The three short ends should, of course, point away from the direction in which the knot is being pulled so that they will not be pulled by the current or catch against any rocks.

1 Make a bight with the working end of one of the two ropes to be joined.

2 Take the end of the other rope and tuck it up through the bight.

3 Pass the working end around and beneath the bight in the other rope.

4 Tuck the end beneath itself so both short ends are on the same side.

5 Then bring the working end around and back on itself again to make a figure-of-eight.

6 Finally, tuck the end beneath itself (as shown) and lay it alongside the two parts of the other rope. Tighten carefully so that all the knot parts bed down snugly together.

Heaving Line Bend

This quick and simple knot attaches a lightweight throwing line (or "messenger") to the bight or eye of a heavier hawser that is to be hauled into position. It was first mentioned in a seamanship manual of 1912.

1 Make a bight in the hawser that has to be hauled.

2 Take the lighter line and lay it over the bight.

3 Divert the working end to one side (the left in this instance), taking it around and beneath the standing part of the bight and then bringing it over its own standing part.

4 Take the working end beneath the short leg of the bight.

5 Bring the working end back to the lefthand side of the knot, tucking it finally beneath itself as shown. Note that the finished shot shows the reverse side of the completed knot.

Racking Bend

1 Make a bight in the larger of the two lines to be temporarily linked and bring the smaller one over it.

2 Divert the working end to one side, tucking it under one leg of the bight.

Racking is the term for figure-of-eight interweaving, such as in this instance, where a small diameter messenger line seizes the bight of a much thicker rope. The purpose is to seize and grip the larger rope so that its bight remains closed and does not spring apart. It is for heavier duties than those undertaken by the various sheet bends, but scale is a relative thing. It can be used to join massive cable-laid cordage aboard ocean-going ships but it could also be applied in fine twines to a model galleon made from matchsticks.

3 Bring the working end back across to the other side, going over, then tucking under the bight.

4 Take the working end back across the bight, going over, then feed it back under again.

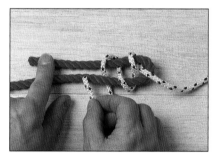

5 Continue this racking process as far along the neck of the bight as necessary to keep it together.

6 Finally, tuck the working end beneath one of the racking turns as shown. The completed knot must be tightened a turn at a time towards the end of the bight.

Seizing Bend

This has all the qualities required of a heaving line bend, namely strength, security and ease of untying. A comparative newcomer on the knotting scene, it was devised and publicized by Harry Asher in 1986.

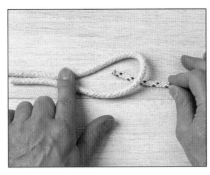

1 Make a bight in the larger of the two lines to be temporarily joined and tuck the end of the lighter line up through it.

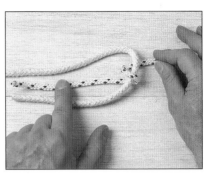

2 Take a turn with the working end of the line around the end of the bight.

3 Divert the working end to one side of the bight and begin to wrap it.

4 Ensure that the first turn traps its preceding standing part.

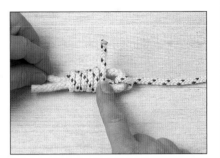

5 Wrap neatly and snugly towards the end of the bight.

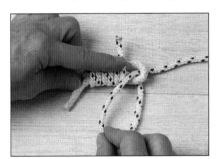

6 Now loosen the initial turn and draw out a loop from it.

7 Pass the loop over the inert end of the bight and pull it tight, so that it holds all of the wrapping turns and traps the working end of the knot. For real security, leave a longer end than shown in the lighter line and fasten it to its own standing part with a bowline.

Albright Special

This tried-and-tested knot is used by numerous anglers to join monofilament to braid, or braid to wire. It is shown here using much thicker cordage than would normally be used. Its first appearance in print was in 1975, but later publications sometimes refer to it as the Allbright Special, so there is some uncertainty as to the correct spelling of the originator's name.

1 Make a bight in the larger of the two lines to be joined.

2 Bring the second line over and parallel with the initial bight.

3 Divert the working end to one side (in this instance the righthand), preparatory to making wrapping turns. Begin the wrapping turns by taking the working end over one side of the bight and back beneath both bight legs.

4 Take the working end back over the top of the bight, trapping its preceding standing part in the process.

5 Continue to wrap over and down beneath the bight legs again.

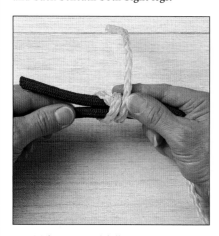

6 Take a second full wrapping turn neatly alongside the first one.

7 Complete as many turns as necessary for a secure and stable knot.

8 Finally, tuck the working end down through the original bight.

Simple Simon Over

This knot (and two variations of it) were devised by Harry Asher and published in 1989. It is especially effective in slick synthetic lines and, once mastered, it can be tied easily. It has rarely appeared in print, but it merits being more widely known as it is a useful knot to have at one's fingertips when faced with tying slippery, synthetic lines.

1 Make a bight in one of the two lines to be joined and bring the working end of the other line over it.

2 Tuck the working end down through the bight and bring it out to the left (in this instance), then take it over both bight legs and, in a snaking "Z" track, back again beneath them.

3 Lay the end back over its preceding part (the "over" of the knot name).

4 From the outside of the bight, tuck the working end up and through and finally lay it alongside its own standing part. Tighten gradually, working the slack out of the completed knot.

Simple Simon Under

This is a variation of the simple Simon over knot by Harry Asher. Although on first appearance, it does not look unlike the simple Simon over, it is more secure and can cope with dissimilar cord sizes and textures. This is an extremely useful knot that deserves more recognition as it is useful for slippery synthetic cord and should be used on a wider scale than it is at present.

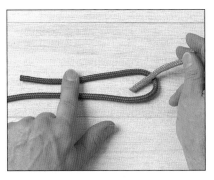

1 Make a bight in one of the two lines to be joined and bring the working end of the other line over it.

2 Tuck the working end down through the bight and divert it to the left (in this instance) prior to going back over both bight legs.

3 Bring the working end back beneath both bight legs and then tuck it beneath its preceding part (the "under" of the knot name).

4 From the outside of the bight, tuck the working end up through and finally lay it alongside its own standing part. Tighten gradually, working the slack out of the completed knot.

Simple Simon Double

This is a variation of the simple Simon knots of Harry Asher; it is even more secure and has the advantage that it can cope with a greater dissimilarity of cord sizes and textures.

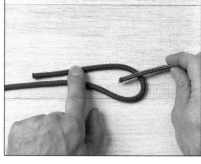

1 Make a bight in the larger of the two lines to be joined and bring the working end of the other line over it.

2 Divert the working end (in this instance taking it to the left) beneath the bight.

3 Wrap the end over and then beneath both bight legs.

4 Take the working end back again so that it lies over both legs of the bight.

5 Pass the working end down beneath the bight over its own preceding standing part.

6 Carry the end across the front of the bight over its own standing part.

7 From the outside of the bight, finally tuck the working end through alongside its own standing part. Pull the knot snug and tight, taking care not to distort it in the process.

Shake Hands

This excellent knot is almost unknown, yet it is one of the best bends, being not only secure but also easily loosened and untied, and neat in appearance with the ends alongside the standing parts. Harry Asher devised it, influenced – admittedly – by Clifford Ashley's 1944 description of a similar layout as a loop knot.

1 Make a loop with one working end going over its own standing part.

2 Pass the other working end up through the initial loop and make a second loop (the end going under the standing part).

3 Take the first working end back down behind both of the loops in the developing knot.

4 Bring the first working end up through the common central space between both loops.

5 Now bring the first working end down in front of both loops.

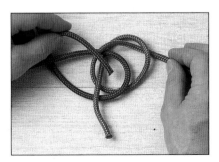

6 Then tuck the second working end down through the common central space between both of the loops.

7 Pull on both working ends and standing parts in turn to tighten the knot.

Tumbling Thief Knot, Centre-tucked

This chunky knot, with both ends centrally nipped, is a good reason to learn the unreliable common thief knot described below.

1 Make a bight in one of the two lines to be joined. Bring the working end of the other line up through the bight and then divert it to the side of the bight where its short end is located.

2 Bring the working end down beneath both legs of the bight, and tuck the end back through the initial bight alongside its own standing part. This is the common thief knot.

3 Now begin to pull each of the working ends across to the opposite side of the knot.

4 Uncross the working cords to momentarily assume the loosely locked layout shown.

5 Cross the two working ends over precisely as shown. This is the tumbling thief, a relatively secure form of the thief knot if drawn tight.

6 Take the upper working end and tuck it directly down through the common central space of the existing knot.

7 Take the lower working end and tuck it up through the common central space. Pull on each one of the four cords in turn to tighten this knot.

Alpine Butterfly Bend

Cutting the loop off an Alpine butterfly knot produces this bend. Indeed, a lot of loop knots can be converted to useful bends this way, and knot tyers who have spotted and reported this principle include Brion Toss, Desmond Mandeville and Harry Asher. Tie it directly to bend together two lines.

1 Form an underhand loop with one of the two ends to be joined.

2 Form a similar underhand loop with the other end, interlocking it with the first loop, as shown.

3 Take either one of the two working ends and tuck it down through the central space common to both loops.

4 Then tuck the other working end down beside the first end, through the almost completed knot.

5 Pull gently on both working ends, then on the standing parts, to remove slack and tighten the knot.

Bowline Bend

In wet natural fibre ropes at sea, when even simple knots could be relied upon to hold, it was recommended that hawsers should be joined with a pair of interlocked bowlines, and that still holds good – literally – in some of today's cordage. The advantage of the bowline is that it does not slip or jam even under tension. This bend can be used for lines of dissimilar diameters, constructions and materials, but the two loops may be weakened where their interlinked elbows cross and rub against one another.

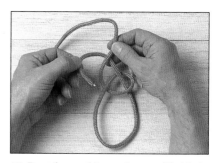

1 Make the initial overhand loop that will cinch the completed knot and tuck the working end up through it.

2 Pass the working end around behind the standing part of the line.

3 Tuck the working end down through the loop and pull the working end to tighten the knot.

4 Make an overhand loop with a second line and tuck the working end through the first bowline.

5 Pass the working end up through the second loop and under the standing part of the line.

6 Tuck this working end down through the second loop and pull the working end to tighten the knot.

Twin Bowline Bend

This alternative to the bowline bend avoids the sharp elbows of the latter knot and is stronger for that reason as it avoids the risk of chafing and rubbing.

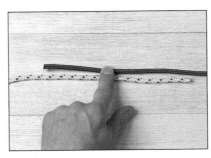

1 Arrange the two lines parallel, with the working ends opposed.

2 Form the loop that is characteristic of bowlines in the standing part of one of the lines, as shown.

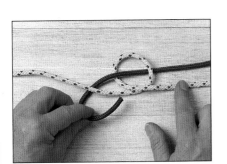

3 Tuck the other working end up through the loop and pass it around the back of the standing part.

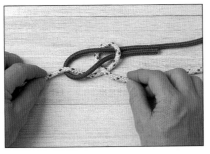

4 Tuck the end down through the loop to complete the first bowline.

5 Turn the half-completed knot end-for-end and begin again with an identical loop.

6 Take the end and tuck it as before, up through the loop and around the standing part.

7 Tuck the end down through the loop to complete the second bowline, ensuring that the working ends are at least as long as those illustrated (and preferably longer). The standing parts will each take an equal part of the strain upon the loaded knot.

HITCHES

"Hitches are employed in making fast to such things as a pile, bitt, spar, rail, ring or hook, and . . . no one hitch will suffice for all."

(Hervey Garrett Smith – *The Arts of the Sailor*, 1953)

A line is said to be "made fast" (not "hitched") to various objects, even another rope, and only the knot itself is called a hitch. Some hitches work best with a direct pull at right angles to the point of attachment; others will withstand a sideways or varying direction of pull; it is a rare and remarkable hitch indeed that can cope with a pull towards the point of a tapering foundation – but one is included in this section. The fisherman's or anchor bend and the gaff topsail halyard bend are actually hitches and so are included within this section. Their irregular names are due to old-time sailormen who, obeying a verbal quirk, always spoke of "bending" a line to a ring or spar. The ossel knot is also a hitch, but it is known as a knot since there is already an ossel hitch.

Pedigree Cow Hitch

This is a useful knot for a pull that is more or less at right angles to the point of attachment. Put it to work to start lashings or to suspend garden shed and garage impedimenta from the roof.

1 Take the working end around and down, from front to back of the anchorage point.

2 Bring the end around in front of its own standing part.

3 Take the end back up behind the foundation and bring it down in front once again.

4 Tuck the end through the bight, the result being a fairly useless common cow hitch.

5 Now tuck the working end back through the basic knot to secure and transform it.

Cow Hitch Variant

This is an even stronger and more secure version than the pedigree cow hitch. Although similar to the pedigree cow hitch, which was an innovation from the fresh mind of Harry Asher, the cow hitch variant was published in 1995 by Robert Pont of France, who first spotted it in Quebec and named it the Piwich knot after the child (Piwich Kust of the Bois Brule tribe) who tied it. Use it as a bag knot, or to suspend lockets, amulets and similar items of jewellery from a neck lanyard.

1 Take the working end once around the point of attachment.

2 Make a single half hitch with the working end around the line's standing part.

3 Take the working end across the front and pass it up (in this instance, to the left) behind the anchorage point.

4 Bring the working end down in front and tuck it down beside the standing part of the line, taking it through the enclosing turn.

Figure-of-Eight Hitch

A trivial holdfast for the odd undemanding job, this hitch is relatively simple and easy to master. The extra crossing point gives a bit more friction and hold than a single half hitch. It is more secure than a single half hitch, especially around an object with a small diameter, and could, of course, be used with a round turn, but always treat it with caution as it does not have the strength of many other hitches.

1 Pass the working end of the line around the anchorage point from front to back.

2 Bring the end forward and across the standing part (in this instance, from right to left).

3 Take the end (in this instance, from left to right) around the back of the standing part.

4 Tuck the end up through the loop to create the characteristic figure-of-eight layout.

Buntline Hitch

In effect, this is two half hitches with the second one inside the first, the working end being trapped against whatever it is tied around. This knot is for situations where the line flaps about with a tendency to shake less secure knots loose (for example, running rigging and flag halyards). A buntline was used to brail up square-sails, which flogged unmercifully, and so a very secure knot was needed. Tied in flat material, it turns out to be the common four-in-hand necktie knot that around 1860 superseded bowties for men.

1 Pass the working end through or around the anchorage point from front to back.

2 Take the end across the front and bring it around the back in a figure of eight layout.

3 Pass the end completely across the loop that has been formed.

4 Continue to take the end around to the back of the arrangement.

5 Tuck the working end through from back to front, as shown, thus forming two half hitches.

Clove Hitch, Tied in a Bight

The ease with which this knot can be tied makes it a popular one, but it comes adrift if pulled and jerked about. Then again, it can also jam, so consider adding a drawloop. Use it to suspend objects by means of lanyards or to secure a light boat to a bollard. Ashore, this knot was once known as a builder's knot.

1 Make an overhand loop at any convenient point in the line.

2 Add an underhand loop further along the line, so that the pair consists of two opposing halves.

3 Arrange the two loops so that they are the same size and close together.

4 Rotate the two loops a little in opposite directions, in order to overlap them.

5 Insert the rail, spar, rope or other foundation through both loops and pull either or both ends to tighten the resulting hitch.

Clove Hitch, Tied with a Working End

When this knot can be neither dropped over a bollard or stanchion nor slipped on to the end of a rail, or it is to be fastened to a ring, it must be tied this way.

1 Pass the working end around the anchorage point from front to back.

2 Bring the end forward and diagonally up across the front of the standing part (in this instance from right to left).

3 Take the working end down the back of the anchorage, so as to trap the standing part.

4 Then tuck the end up beneath the diagonal (forming what looks like a letter N, or its mirror-image).

5 Use a drawloop if an easy quick-release is required. Pull the standing part to tighten the knot.

Ground Line Hitch

This is a simple and easily tied knot to hitch a thin cord on to a thicker one. It is a tried and trusted hitch that has been used by cod fishermen on their trawl nets and as a picket line hitch by horse soldiers and wilderness pioneers. It can be used in the end of a coil of line to keep it all together, and is suitable for all kinds of cordage or other pliable materials. Add a drawloop for quick release, provided the knot is only intended to hold inanimate objects and the pull is a steady one.

1 Pass the working end around the foundation from front to back.

2 Bring the end forward again (in this instance, to the left of its own standing part).

3 Take the working end up and diagonally across the front of the work.

4 Pass the working end down behind the foundation to emerge at the front and to the right of the standing part.

5 Pull up the standing part to create an upper bight.

6 Tuck the working end through the newly created bight and then pull down on the standing part to trap it.

Highwayman's Hitch

Children like to learn and show off this hitch, because of the way its apparent complexity melts to nothing with one tug on the short end. Use it as a third hand for handiwork, as well as to moor or tether a boat or horse. There is no reason to believe that highwaymen ever actually used this knot.

1 Make a bight in one end of a rope, cord or other line and pass it up behind the hitching rail.

2 Pick up the standing part of the line and make a similar second bight at the front of the rail.

3 Tuck the second bight from front to back through the first one, then pull down on the working end to secure it.

4 Make a second bight in the working end (this is the third bight in total).

5 Tuck this third bight from front to back through the second one and finally pull down on the standing part to secure it. The final bight may be loaded; and the working end tugged for quick release.

Rolling Hitch

An elaboration of the clove hitch, this is intended to cope with a lengthwise pull. The two diagonal riding turns must go on the side of the object from which the pull will be applied.

1 Pass the working end around the anchorage from front to back.

2 Take the end up and diagonally across the front of the standing part.

3 Bring the working end down behind the work once more, bringing it out to emerge between the diagonal and the standing part.

4 Create a second diagonal turn, snugly beside the first one (and closest to the standing part), before passing the end down behind the work once more.

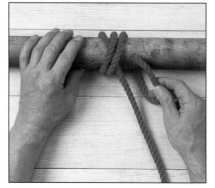

5 Tuck the working end up beneath the last diagonal turn only and lever it tight.

Ossel Hitch

"Ossel" is a Scottish sea fisherman's word (Cornish: "orsel") for a gill net. These knots secured the submerged lower ends of ossel lines that supported the nets as they were towed through choppy seas behind the fishing vessels known as drifters. Subjected to continual underwater movement, this seemingly simple knot coped with it all. It is a super little hitch.

1 Bring the working end down behind the foundation rope and around to the front.

2 Pass the end up and around the back of the standing part (in this instance, from left to right).

3 Take the working end down the front of the foundation rope and then bring it back up behind the work.

4 Finally, tuck the end over the first knot part and then beneath the second (as shown).

Ossel Knot

At the upper end of ossel ropes was this more secure knot which, in contrast to the submerged ossel hitch, had to resist being bashed about on the surface of rough seas.

1 Pass the working end up at the front, then over and down behind the foundation rope.

2 Bring the end up and diagonally across in front of the standing part and put it down behind the work.

3 Bring the working end up alongside the first wrapping turn and take it up for a second, diagonal wrapping turn.

4 Starting on the same side of the standing part, complete the second diagonal, so that it lies snugly beside the first one.

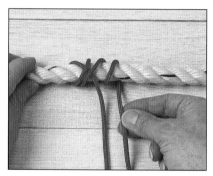

5 Wrap the working end up in front of the foundation rope once more, this time on the far side of the standing part from the two diagonal turns.

6 Pull out a loose bight in the standing part where it passes over the foundation rope.

7 Tuck the working end through the bight from front to back. Trap it by pulling down on the standing part.

Gaff Topsail Halyard Bend

A legacy from the days of wooden ships, tarred ropes and large canvas sails, even the name of this knot evokes an image of blustering storms and sea spray. However, this is a misleading name since this knot is actually a hitch, an oddity that comes from the fact that sailors, by some unwritten rule, always talked of "bending" ropes to rings or spars. It is sufficiently secure under a steady pull at right angles to the point of attachment.

1 Take the working end of the rope or other line up behind the rail or spar and then bring it down in front.

2 Pass the end up behind the anchorage once again, completing a turn.

3 Bring the working end down in front once more, making a full round turn, and take it behind its own standing part.

4 Finally tuck the end up (in this instance from left to right) beneath both parts of the round turn.

Vibration-proof Hitch

The American physicist Amory Bloch Lovins invented this knot over 20 years ago. It is designed for an anchorage of large diameter. Vibration of the standing part will only tighten it further due to the ratchet-like operation of the knot parts.

1 Pass the working end of the cord up, around and down the foundation from front to back, then take it diagonally up and to the right (in this instance) beneath its own standing part.

2 Take the end once more up, over and down behind the foundation.

3 Take the end across the front of the standing part then through the underlying diagonal (from left to right).

4 Go over the overlaying knot part and finally tuck the end beneath the diagonal again. Pull intermittently upon the standing part to tighten this knot.

Snuggle Hitch

This relatively new knot, which came to notice in 1987, was created by Owen K. Nuttall of West Yorkshire, England. Extra tucks and turns yield added security to withstand a variable pull in even synthetic cordage.

1 Take a turn with the working end and then leave it diagonally up and across the front of the standing part.

2 Pass the end down the back of the anchorage and bring it up at the front again.

3 Lead the working end across in front of the standing part to tuck it under its own previous pass.

4 Take the working end down behind the anchorage once again.

5 Lead the end over one knot part and tuck it beneath the next.

6 Take the working end down behind the work yet again, bringing it up at the front to go over one knot part and finally tuck beneath the next.

95

Boom Hitch

This attractive and robust hitch, described by Clifford Ashley in 1944, is quickly and easily tied with consecutive wrapping turns, and just a final single tuck to secure it. It really would, as the name suggests, cope with the variable direction and strength of pull involved as an improvised main sheet on a sailing dinghy, and it works equally well whether wet or dry.

1 Lay the working end diagonally up and across (in this instance, from left to right) the anchorage point.

2 Take the end down behind the anchorage and bring it under and forward again.

3 Lead the working end diagonally up and across its own standing part from right to left.

4 Take the end down again behind the anchorage and bring it forward.

5 Make a diagonal pass with the working end up and across from left to right over the intervening knot part.

6 Pass the end down behind the work between the two existing knot parts, to emerge at the front.

7 Take the end diagonally up from right to left over the standing end and one knot part.

8 Pass the working end down behind the anchorage to emerge at the front once again.

9 Make a final diagonal pass with the working end up from left to right, going over one knot part and tucking beneath the next. Make snug and tight.

Timber Hitch / Killick Hitch

The timber hitch is used by logging contractors to haul felled tree trunks from the undergrowth to the nearest transportation, although it will retrieve and drag all sorts of inanimate objects over rough terrain or through water.

For long and thin loads, such as scaffold poles or grounded flagmasts, an added half hitch (converting the initial timber hitch to a killick hitch) keeps them moving in a straight line. Because a "killick" was the naval name for a light anchor, rock or anything else that might hold a small boat on the sea or riverbed, a killick hitch was originally a rough-and-ready attachment for a boat, mooring buoy or even a lobster pot.

1 Pass the working end of a line up around the object to be towed and bring it to the front.

2 Take the end around its own standing part and make a small loop.

3 Tuck the working end through between the standing end and itself.

4 Bring the end around and repeat steps 2 – 3 to make a similar second tuck between the standing end and itself.

5 Complete the second tuck (adding a third and fourth if the diameter of the load and the cordage require the extra friction). Improvising a sliding noose in this way is known as "dogging".

6 Pull on the standing end to tighten the newly formed noose around the load. This is the basic timber hitch.

7 Make a half-hitch with the working end to convert a timber hitch into a killick hitch.

8 Locate the half-hitch away from the initial knot – perhaps a metre (about a yard) or more, depending on the scale of the job – to ensure a pull along the length of the load.

Clinging Clara

When the need arises to attach a thin line to a thicker rope for a lengthwise pull, this hitch really grips and holds. It is another creation by Harry Asher, dating from about 1989. The load must be applied to the standing part, which is on the right in the step pictures (taken upwards in the finished shot). Be prudent. Leave a longer working end than the one illustrated in the step-by-step tying shots.

1 Take a turn with the working end of the smaller line around the larger rope, in the direction of the strands if it is hawser-laid.

2 Bring the working end back towards the standing part of the thinner line.

3 Lead the working end across in front of the standing part, then around behind it, to return and pass over its own previous part.

4 Take the working end (in this instance, from right to left) over one knot part, finally tucking it beneath the initial turn.

Lighterman's Hitch

River Thames tugmen tow the Port of London's heavy dumb barges (lighters) with this strong, yet versatile hitch. It has also proved its worth with riggers in circus and theatre, as well as stevedores (longshoremen), being a heavy-duty professional holdfast that would support the weight of a massive marquee or berth an ocean liner. Yet, because this hitch never completely tightens, it is remarkably adaptable as it can be cast off effortlessly in seconds.

5 Bring the working end over the top of the standing part, creating a small loop around it.

6 Take a turn around the post or peg with the working end.

1 Pass the working end of the tow line or guy line around the post or peg.

3 Take hold of the working end (which must be fairly long) and pull out a bight from it.

2 Complete a round turn, using the friction gained to check or snub the load, and adjust the rope or other line to the required length.

4 Bring the bight beneath the taut standing part of the line and place it over the towing post, tent peg or other anchorage point.

Knute Hitch

This simple, and no doubt ancient, knot was named by American master rigger Brion Toss in 1990. It attaches a lanyard or halyard to anything with a small eye, so safeguarding objects such as pocket knives or other tools, securing a sail or fastening a curtain tie-back.

1 Make a small bight in the working end of the lanyard.

2 Push the bight through any hole that is barely bigger than the doubled cord.

3 Tuck the end (with a stopper knot added to it) through the bight and pull on the standing part to tighten.

Pile Hitch

Little known – and often not considered a "proper" knot – this simple hitch is tied more quickly than it can be described. It is ideal for attaching barrier ropes to posts and rails where the bight or loop can be passed over the top, for crowd control or to isolate road works. John Smith, an active member of the The International Guild of Knot Tyers, suggests that, if there were to be only one knot in the world, it would have to be this one – for it can (as he demonstrates) also be ingeniously adapted into a knot, bend, binding or loop.

1 Make a bight at any selected point in the rope or line.

2 Pass the bight beneath both standing parts, and loop it over the post, stanchion or peg. Both legs of the line may then be led in different directions.

Double Pile Hitch

John Smith devised this double pile hitch as an alternative to the rolling hitch to enable a lengthways pull.

1 Make a bight at any selected point in the rope or cord.

2 Pass the bight around the post, stanchion, peg or other item used as an anchorage point.

3 Take the bight beneath the two standing parts to make a turn.

4 Lead the bight further around the anchorage to complete a round turn.

5 Bring the bight beneath both standing parts and pass it over the anchorage. This hitch is designed to cope with a load from one or both of the standing parts and towards the bight.

Icicle Hitch

As an extension of his double pile hitch, John Smith first demonstrated this astonishng contrivance in May 1990 at the eighth Annual General Meeting of the International Guild of Knot Tyers, when he hung suspended by it from a splicing fid (tapered point down). As this demonstration proved, with careful arrangement this hitch will hold a considerable load on the smoothest of foundations – even a fireman's brass pole would be suitable. It has recently received fulsome praise from a civil engineer, who used it to lever a young tree out of the ground, after previous efforts by other means had failed and left the tree stripped of its bark and consequently slippery and smooth.

1 Lead the working end of the line over and around the foundation from front to back.

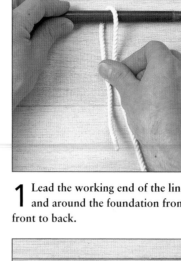

2 Take a round turn with the working end, working away from the direction of intended pull.

3 Create at least four turns, or more if an exceptionally secure hitch is required.

4 Drape the working end over the end of the foundation, as shown, with a bight hanging down at the back.

5 Bring the bight up in front of all the wrapping turns and both ends of the line, then pass it over the end of the foundation. Tighten everything by pulling each end in turn at right angles to the spar. Then tighten it again. Carefully apply the load, so that the knot stretches out (as illustrated). The final two turns – on the thicker part, if there is a taper – must not separate; if they do, add extra turns; once they remain together, the hitch should hold.

Bale Sling Hitch

This arrangement of an endless cargo strop will sling a sack, cask or any other load that is squat, round and inert. If a crane or other derrick is used, the upper bight would be put on to the hook with a cat's paw.

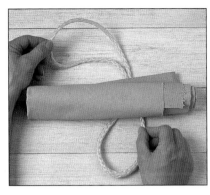

1 Lay the rope or webbing strop or sling beneath the load that is to be lifted.

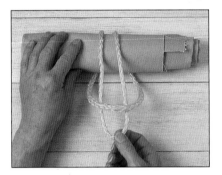

2 Pass the bight that forms one end of the strop through the other end.

3 Pull up on the working bight to tighten the hitch; then simply release the load to loosen it again.

Ring Hitch

To attach any object – a knife, lucky mascot or other ornament – to a lanyard loop, use this hitch. If the loop is pre-tied in the lanyard, then it is obviously essential that the loop is long enough to pass over whatever is to be suspended from it.

1 Double a cord and pass the bight thus formed through the eye of the object to be attached.

2 Spread the bight wide enough to pass over the item on which it is being knotted.

3 Pull evenly upon both standing parts of the cord to tighten the hitch.

Cat's Paw

A strong hook or ring hitch for a heavy load, this strop hitch is used by stevedores (long-shoremen) in big hawsers and by anglers in considerably finer lines. Hanging double parts of loaded rope over a hook lessens the chance of it weakening. The cat's paw, when drawn up tightly, provides extra security. If, by chance, one leg of the rope should accidentally break, the other may take the weight of the load and enable the cargo to be lowered slowly to the ground, rather than allowing it to fall from a greater height.

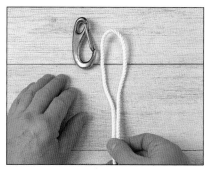

1 Make a bight in an endless strop or double a length of line.

2 Bend the bight over to create a pair of matching loops.

3 Twist both loops, the lefthand one clockwise and the righthand in the opposite direction.

4 Continue until three or four twists have accumulated, with exactly the same number on each loop.

5 Insert the hook or other anchorage through both of the twisted loops.

6 Pull evenly on both standing parts to straighten them and slide the wrapping turns that result up snug to the hook or other fixture.

Anchor Bend

Related to the round turn and
two half hitches, this even more
secure hitch is used when a line is
wet and slippery (such as one
attached to the ring of a small
boat's anchor). Because old-time
sailormen "bent" a rope to an
anchor or a spar, the hitches they
used for this particular purpose
acquired the contradictory and
misleading name of "bends". This
example is also known as the
fisherman's bend.

1 Pass the working end of the line
through the ring.

2 Lead the working end through the
ring a second time, then bring it
back to the standing part, completing a
round turn.

3 Tuck the working end through the
round turn and tie a half hitch.

4 Tie an identical second half hitch,
leaving a longer end than illustrated.
If a semi-permanent hitch is desirable, tape
or tie it to the standing part of the line.

Anchor Bend Variant

This neat variant of the anchor bend was anonymously published back in 1904. It is effectively a round turn within a round turn, and it is snug, compact and secure.

1 Pass the working end of the line through the ring.

2 Lead the end through the ring a second time to create a round turn.

3 Tuck the working end through the round turn previously formed.

4 Then tuck the end a second time to create what is in effect one round turn through another round turn.

Halter Hitch

As with the highwayman's hitch, this knot is used, as its name implies, to tether animals. This is also a general-purpose hitch. Be warned, however, that some horses may chew on knots like this and ultimately undo them with their teeth.

1 Lead the working end through or around the anchorage point to cross its own standing part and form a loop.

2 Pass the end around and behind (in this instance, from left to right) to form a second loop beneath the first.

3 Make a bight in the working end and tuck it to tie a running overhand knot with drawloop.

4 Tighten the knot and adjust the sliding loop, then finish off by tucking the end through the drawloop to secure it.

Half Blood Knot

Anglers use this knot to attach a line to a hook, lure or swivel. Pull on the standing part of the line to convert the twists into snug wrapping turns.

1 Pass the working end through the ring that is the point of attachment.

2 Begin to twist the working end and the standing part together.

3 Continue the twisting process, ensuring an even tension on both parts of the line.

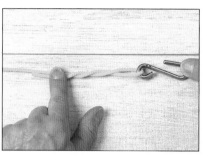

4 Make five or six twists, working away from the ring.

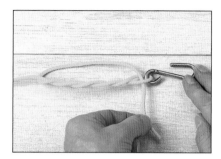

5 Bring the working end over and tuck it down through the loop, trapping it alongside the ring.

Mooring Hitch

In a tideway, where small boats rise and fall at their berths, take a mooring painter around a post and tie this slide-and-lock knot. Its versatility is particularly suited to mooring as you can adjust it whenever necessary to match the length of the painter to the changing water level. It can be readily released from the craft itself, if the drawloop is made in a long line that is taken back on board.

1 Pass the working end of a line around the point the boat is to be moored to.

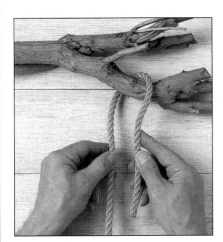

2 With the end, make an underhand loop and lay it on top of the standing part of the line.

3 Make a bight in the working end (which can be left long or kept short, as required).

4 Lead the bight over-under-over the loop and standing part, in a locking tuck, to create a drawloop.

Palomar Knot

This is a strong knot, claimed by some to be 95 to 100 per cent efficient. It can be used to attach a bight securely to an angler's arbor, or to a hook, lure, swivel or sinker.

1 Pass the end of a loop (or a bight of line) through the ring.

2 Bring the bight back across itself to form a doubled loop.

3 Then tuck the bight through the loop to tie an overhand knot around the ring.

4 Push the ring itself down through the bight in the line.

5 Then carry the bight back clear over the knot parts.

Jansik Special

This is another very strong attachment (some anglers claim that it is 95 to 100 per cent) for hook, line or swivel. The double turn through the ring gives additional strength, while the triple tuck with the tag end lends security to this compact knot. It is worth perfecting this knot on thicker cord before trying to tie it in nylon monofilament.

1 Pass the working end through the ring and under the standing part.

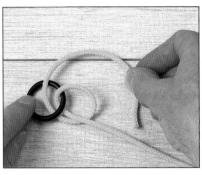

2 Lead the end through the ring a second time to create a round turn.

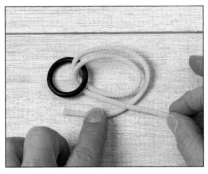

3 Take the working end beneath the standing part of the line.

4 Take a wrapping turn with the working end to enclose the two earlier turns that include the standing part.

5 Tuck the working end through the loop a second time, taking care to wrap away from the ring.

6 Complete three or four turns before carefully removing all of the slack to tighten the knot.

Turle Knot

For angled or offset eyed hooks and flies, this classic anglers' knot was published in 1841 and later popularized by Major Turle of Newton Stacey in Hampshire, England. Since a few people have now begun mistakenly to call it the turtle knot, this puts the record straight.

1 Pass the working end of the monofilament or braid through the eye of the hook or other object.

2 Lead the end around the shank of the hook and across the standing part to form a loop.

3 Tuck the end to create a short-lived half hitch.

4 Then finally tuck the working end to tie an overhand knot.

True Lover's Knot

One of the weaker angling knots (50 to 70 per cent), this hitch attaches monofilament or braided plastic-coated wire to a lure.

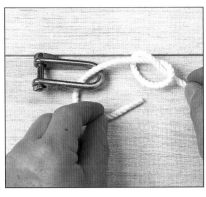

1 Tie an overhand knot and then pass the working end through the ring.

2 Tuck the end back through the knot alongside the standing part.

3 Adjust the ring loop to the required size; a small loop will allow the lure freedom to move realistically.

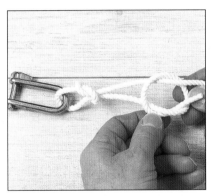

4 Tie a twin overhand knot with the working end, around the standing part of the line.

5 Arrange the second knot so that it lies snugly embedded against the first knot, then pull on the standing end to tighten the entire assembly.

KNOTS

The word "knot" has a specific meaning,
apart from its general use for any cordage
entanglement. Strictly speaking, it refers
only to those that are not bends or hitches,
namely stopper knots, shortenings, loops and
bindings, as well as anything tied in string
or other small stuff, such as cotton or thread.
Stopper cordage knots may be used to prevent
fraying (when a whipping cannot be applied
immediately) but their function is primarily
to prevent the cord pulling out of a pulley-
block, fairlead or other opening. Shortenings
are temporary devices, intended
to avoid cutting rope that must later be reused.
Loops may be single or multiple, fixed or
sliding. Bindings can be makeshift quick
seizings or semi-permanent lashings,
while slide-and-grip knots are remarkable
shock-absorbing contrivances.

Ashley's Stopper Knot

The overhand knot, figure-of-eight knot and stevedore knot, despite their increasing bulks, will all pull through a hole of about the same diameter. For a fatter stopper, use this knot devised by Clifford Ashley sometime around 1910 after he had spied a lumpy knot, which he did not recognize, aboard a boat in the local oyster fishing fleet. This was the outcome, hence his name for it (the oysterman's stopper knot). Later, when he was able to see the mystery knot close up, it proved to be nothing but a wet and badly swollen figure-of-eight knot; but Ashley's new stopper knot has survived to become a minor classic.

1 Immobilizing the end, throw an overhand loop in the standing part of the line.

2 Take the standing part of the line beneath the loop.

3 Pull a bight through the loop to create an overhand knot with a drawloop.

4 Bring the working end up and through from the back of the bight (no other way will do). Pull the standing part down until the bight traps the end tightly against the knot.

Figure-of-Eight Knot

Favoured by dinghy sailors for the ends of jib leads and main sheets, this quick and simple knot has a bit more bulk than an overhand knot and is more easily untied – but it will escape through holes of roughly the same size. In its untightened form, this familiar knot has long been associated with faithful love – an emblem of interwoven affection.

1 Make a small bight at the end of the line and impart half a twist to turn it into a loop.

2 Impart an extra half twist to bring about the figure-of-eight shape that gives this knot its name.

3 Begin to pull the working end through the loop from the top. If you wish to leave a drawloop, stop at this stage.

4 Draw the working end right the way through to complete a common figure-of-eight knot. To tighten this knot, tug first on both ends to remove slack from the knot; then pull on just the standing part, pulling the end over and trapping it against the top of the knot.

Stevedore's Knot

Prior to the advent of container craft, stevedores (longshoremen) worked aboard ships to load and unload cargoes piecemeal. Between them, they hoisted sacks, crates and casks in and out of warehouses by means of a rope through a single pulley, and this knot stopped it from coming free.

1 Make a small bight at one end of the line and give this bight half a twist to create a loop.

2 Add another half-twist to the bight to make interlocked elbows from the initial loop.

3 Add yet another half-twist, one beyond the making of a figure-of-eight knot.

4 Then, add a final half-twist (the fourth) to complete the preparation of this knot.

5 Tuck the working end up through the loop and carefully pull out all the slack, in this way encircling the standing part of the line and trapping the working end against the body of the knot with the bight.

Crossing Knot

It could be argued that this is actually one of the simplest and most insecure of hitches, although it is rarely, if ever, classified that way in knot manuals. In fact it is inconsistencies like these that make knot lore such a fascinating field of study for devotees. Use this to brace parcel ties or to suspend a barrier rope from stake to stake at a school fete; even plastic tape at a scene of crime might be hitched from tree to lampost to railing by means of this knot. (It is also the basis for the harness bend.)

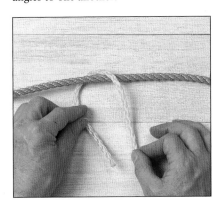

1 Cross one line over the other line or the post so that they are at right angles to one another.

2 Bring the working end back down behind the other line.

3 Take the working end across the front (from left to right in this example) of its own standing part.

4 Tuck the end up and under the other line. Tension must be maintained, since there is no locking tuck to retain the form of this arrangement.

Prusik Knot

Dr Karl Prusik, an Austrian professor of music, originally devised this knot during the First World War to mend the broken strings of musical instruments. Then, in 1931, he published instructions for mountaineers as to how it might be used for self-rescue. With downward pressure, the knot jams, but when the weight is removed, it frees itself and can be pushed up the rope. The original knot has been largely superseded by many other slide-and-grip knots, all now referred to as prusiking knots.

1 Make a bight with part of an endless sling. Lay this over a climbing rope.

2 Bend the bight over and down behind the climbing rope.

3 Pass the standing part of the sling through the working bight.

4 Pull some slack out of the initial bight and take it up and over the rope once more.

5 Take the working bight back down behind the climbing rope again.

6 Tuck the remainder of the standing part through the wrapped bight and tighten the knot.

Double Prusik Knot

In icy or muddy conditions, you need to insure against slippage and modify the basic prusik knot with another wrap or two. As with the prusik knot, this can be used in pairs on one piece of rope so that it is possible to work your way up a line by alternating the weight between the two knots. Always tie the knot with cord that is smaller than the main rope it is being tied around. The double prusik knot can be adapted into an eight-wrap (triple prusik) knot – simply repeat steps 1–3.

1 Tie a basic prusik knot and pull some slack from the working bight.

2 Wrap the slack from the bight up and over the climbing rope.

3 Tuck the working bight down behind the rope to add an extra pair of wrapping turns. Tuck the working loop down through to complete the knot.

4 Tighten the result into a six-wrap version of the basic four-wrap knot. Repeat steps 1 – 3 to produce an eight-wrap (triple prusik) knot.

Bachmann Knot

Used with a karabiner, this knot can be moved more easily than the original prusik knot. It is the oldest of the so-called semi-mechanical knots that rely for their function upon the incorporation of climbing hardware.

1 Make a bight in part of an endless sling or strop.

2 Clip a karabiner into the bight, and then pass the sling behind the climbing rope.

3 Start to seize the karabiner to the rope with a wrapping turn made in the sling.

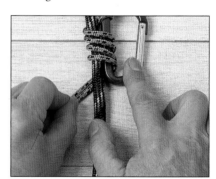

4 Add further wrapping turns, keeping them neatly alongside one another.

5 Continue to wrap until the karabiner is full (but not overfull).

Klemheist Knot

This knot may also be formed around a karabiner (not illustrated), which makes it easier to shift when prusiking.

1 Make a bight in part of an endless strop or sling.

2 Begin to wrap the sling upwards around the climbing rope.

3 Continue to create wrapping turns with the sling around the rope.

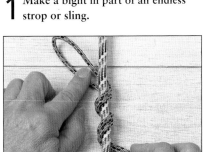

4 Ensure that both legs of the sling remain flat and parallel, with no crossovers, as the wrapping proceeds.

5 Complete four or five turns with the sling around the rope.

6 Tighten and neaten the wrapping turns (not perfectly illustrated) and bring the working bight down to the standing part of the sling.

7 Tuck the remainder of the sling through the working bight to complete this friction hitch.

Mariner's Knot

To take the weight of a fallen climber off the belay device, a sling with a mariner's knot is attached to the anchors (and a klemheist to the climbing rope). The knot can be released under load, and works best with 1.4 cm/$^7/_{12}$ in to 1.7 cm/$^7/_{10}$ in webbing. It is, presumably, named after its originator and has no nautical use.

1 Make a flattened bight in a webbing sling of appropriate width for the size of karabiner.

2 Pass the webbing bight over and through the appropriate karabiner.

3 Tuck the sling through the karabiner a second time to create a round turn.

4 Bring the working end of the sling around the front of the standing part.

5 Wrap it around the back of the standing part of the sling.

6 Wrap a second, third and fourth turn around the standing part.

7 Finally, tuck the working end of the sling between the two flat legs of the standing part. Friction and tension alone secure this hitch.

Penberthy Knot

Devised by Larry Penberthy and Dick Mitchell in about 1969, this prusiking knot is also known as the caver's helical knot. As it can be fiddly to tie, climbing writer Bill March suggests a sling weighted with a karabiner twirled around the rope, and the sling then threaded through it, makes tying much easier. Always adjust the number of turns and the amount of slack to the user's weight; too much slack and it slips, too little and it becomes difficult to shift.

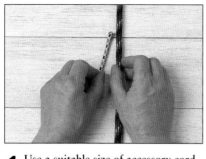

1 Use a suitable size of accessory cord for the climbing rope.

2 Begin to wrap turns around the rope; it may not matter whether the turns go up (as illustrated) or down.

3 Wrap the accessory cord a second time around the climbing rope.

4 Continue until five or six wrapping turns have been completed.

5 Make an overhand loop in the upper one of the two cords.

6 Then take the lower cord and tuck it through this loop.

7 Take the working end (lower end of the cord) around the upper cord of the half-completed knot.

8 Tuck the end down through the loop to secure the arrangement with a sheet bend.

Munter Friction Hitch

An effective means of abseiling (rappelling), belaying or absorbing the energy of a fall, this friction hitch for kernmantel rope also reverses to yield slack or apply tension when needed. The rope is pressed around and through the karibiner and will break the fall of a climber by locking up, in much the same way that a car seat belt locks. Although it can be used for abseiling (rappelling), this is not generally recommended as the practice can be hard on the rope, eventually causing it to "burn". The munter friction hitch was introduced in 1974, and is also known as the Italian hitch and sliding ring hitch.

1 Use the climbing rope with an appropriate size and quality of karabiner.

2 Make a loop (exactly as illustrated) in the climbing rope.

3 Unscrew (if necessary) and open the gate of the karabiner.

4 Hook upwards with the karabiner to incorporate the climbing rope.

5 Then pass the karabiner through the initial loop from back to front (no other way will work).

6 When completed, this hitch is revealed as a dynamic crossing knot. The finished shot shows this knot from the rear side.

Double Munter Friction Hitch

Canadian rock and building climber Robert Chisnall devised and publicized this variation of the munter friction hitch. The additional turn around the karabiner creates greater friction and consequently more control over the load line. This is ideal for smaller diameter rope, which often needs more friction.

1 Choose an appropriate size and quality of karabiner to use with the climbing rope.

2 Make a double loop in the climbing rope, exactly as illustrated.

3 Hook upwards with the karabiner to incorporate the climbing rope.

4 Then pass the karabiner through the initial double loop from back to front as shown (no other way will work).

5 When completed, this hitch exerts more friction, and so will support greater loads than the basic knot.

Munter Mule

A rescuer's "extra hand", this contrivance may be a newcomer to the climbing scene. Ensure you try it out in training situations before resorting to it in trickier circumstances. Used for tying off an injured climber temporarily, this holdfast has the advantage that it can be untied while loaded. It is, in effect, a munter friction hitch – that dynamic relation of the inactive crossing knot – which has been immobilized by the addition of a slip knot backed up by an overhand knot (both tied in the bight). The munter mule's bulkiness makes it easy to undo.

1 Begin with a munter friction hitch tied on to a karabiner, and make a bight with the working end of the rope.

2 Pass the bight just made behind the standing part of the rope.

3 Bring the bight around to the front of the rope and tuck it down through its own loop.

4 Tighten the resulting overhand knot around the standing part of the rope. This is the munter mule.

5 Now take the working bight across the front of the rope, and return the bight around the back of the rope.

6 Finally tuck the working bight through its latest loop to reinforce it with a two-strand overhand knot around the standing part of the rope.

Sheepshank

The sheepshank temporarily shortens a length of rope. It will bridge an obviously damaged or a suspect section of rope, taking the strain upon the other two standing parts.

1 Fold the rope and fold it again, shortening it as required, into a flattened "S" or "Z" shape with two bights.

2 Make an incomplete overhand knot – known as a marlinespike hitch – in one standing part.

3 Pull the adjacent bight through the marlinespike hitch in a locking tuck that goes over-under-over the rope.

4 Turn the half-finished knot end-for-end and make another marlinespike hitch in the other standing part.

5 Insert the remaining bight over-under-over, securing the nearby hitch, and gently tighten both ends of the knot until they are snug and firm. Ensure that the load falls equally on all three standing parts (unless one is damaged, in which case it must lie between the other two and be slightly slacker than them).

Heddon Knot

This knot, which was invented by Chet Heddon in 1959, is also referred to as a cross-prusik knot and as a kreuzklem. It is rated about as effective as the original prusik knot, is harder to loosen and may be tied in either accessory cord or webbing. Avoid tying it upside down or it will slip and not hold. This knot seems to be used only by climbers, but there is no reason why it should not be adopted for mundane use on level ground.

1 Make a bight in a cord or webbing sling and use single or doubled climbing rope.

2 Pass the sling bight behind the climbing rope, then bring it back in front of it.

3 Wrap the other end of the sling across the front of its own bight and around the back of the rope.

4 Finally, tuck the longer sling bight down through the initial bight.

Double Heddon Knot

This elaboration of the basic Heddon, cross-prusik or kreuzklem knot generates greater friction and so may be expected to cope with a greater load. The extra wrap of this beefed-up version of the heddon gives it a slightly different appearance, and this makes it somewhat harder to loosen before it can fulfil its slide-and-grip role, but it is nevertheless a useful variation.

1 Make a bight in a cord or webbing sling and use single or doubled climbing rope.

2 Pass the bight behind the rope, then wrap the remainder of the sling around the rope to trap the bight. Take the sling round to the back of the rope.

3 Wrap the long end of the sling across the front of its own bight a second time and take it once more around the back of the rope.

4 Finally, tuck the longer sling bight down through the initial bight.

Release Hitch, Top Loaded

To overcome the shortcomings of other prusiking knots, Robert Chisnall came up with this innovation around 1980. A weight on the load end causes the turns around the abseil (rappel) line to tighten and the knot to grip. A sharp tug on the release end causes first the top and then the other wrapping turns to slide. Care must be taken in tying this knot as, if it is at all sloppy or loose, it will slip before jamming and may fail.

1 Tie figure-of-eight loops in both ends of a length of cord. Arrange one end, knot down, alongside the climbing rope; then make an overhand loop with the other end.

2 Take the working end around the back of the rope and bring it up through its own loop.

3 Make another wrapping turn with the working end around the rope and up through the loop.

4 Complete as many wrapping turns as may be necessary for the required friction, then pull on the lower end to tighten the knot.

Release Hitch, Bottom Loaded

The bottom loaded version of this hitch, by contrast, is more secure than the prusik knot. It will grip even when sloppily tied, although it tends to drift apart when loaded if there is any slack. The trade-off is that the release end then has to be pulled very hard to make it slip. When tied neatly, the bottom loaded release hitch can be freed more easily.

1 Tie figure-of-eight loops in both ends of a length of accessory cord.

2 Arrange one end of the cord, knot down, alongside the climbing rope; then make an overhand loop as shown with the other end.

3 Lead the working end of the accessory cord around the back of the climbing rope.

4 Tuck the working end up through its earlier loop from front to back, and lead it around behind the rope.

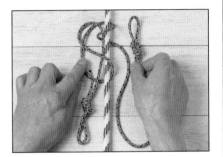

5 Make the first of several wrapping turns to enclose both the cord and rope together.

6 Complete as many wrapping turns as necessary for the required friction.

7 Bring the working end out through the knot as shown and pull upon the unused end to tighten it.

Extended French Prusik Knot

This is another Robert Chisnall innovation from around 1981. It is a sort of Chinese finger trap, in which the extension brought about by a load reduces its diameter, so that it clings to the rope around which it is wrapped. To shift it by hand, grasp the upper end and pull down, thus shortening it and increasing its diameter, so that it releases its grip and slides. In fact, it is intentional that this knot slides under a shock loading as it absorbs energy until the falling load is low enough for the sling and rope to withstand, when it will grip and hold, thus making it ideal for climbers. This tape knot works equally well on a single or doubled climbing rope.

1 Middle a length of 25 mm/1 in tubular tape and arrange it with the bight around the climbing rope.

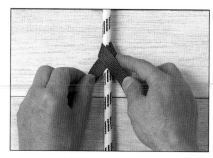

2 Lead both ends in opposite spirals around the rope, crossing one over the other when they meet.

3 Take both working lengths around to the back of the rope, where the one that went over at the previous crossing point now goes under.

4 Bring the tapes around to the front again, alternating the crossover once more.

5 Continue with this over-under-over wrapping of the tape around the rope.

6 Keep the diamond spaces between the tapes as small as possible.

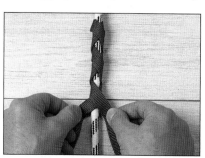

7 Eight or ten wrapping turns are sufficient for this innovative knot.

8 Tie a pair of figure-of-eight loops as close to the rope as possible to be held by a karabiner.

Chi-Fi Knot

This variation of the extended French prusik knot, named after Canadian climbers Robert Chisnall and Jean-Marc Filion, is tied in an endless sling. It frees the user's hands for abseil (rappel) and rescue work. It is a close relation of the extended French prusik knot, also devised by Robert Chisnall. This clever slide-and-grip knot appeared first in the 1989 *Safety Manual* of the Ontario Rock Climbing Association, and may be unknown outside its membership. It is nevertheless a remarkable friction device that could prove useful in all kinds of situations. Aboard boats, the karabiner could be replaced by a shackle and pin. NOTE – This knot glazes slings, losing friction. Retire if glazing is apparent, and in any case after 10 to 12 uses in this way.

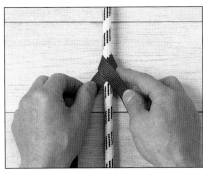

1 Place a tape sling around the climbing rope (which may be single or doubled), crossing one length of rope over the other.

2 Take both sections of tape around to the back of the rope, alternating the crossover.

3 Continue to wrap the tapes, with alternating crossovers, ensuring that the diamond spaces between the tapes are kept as small as possible.

4 Wrap the tapes until all of the slack in the sling is used up.

5 Neaten the lower half of the knot, until it matches the top half, and clip a karabiner through the two remaining bights.

Square Knot

Dressing gown (bath robe) cords or other waist-ties may be fastened with this knot, allowing the ends to hang down stylishly. It is best, however, in a knotted scarf, when the four-panelled knot neatly fills the V-shaped space in an open blouse or shirt. Because there is already a square knot in the United States (which the British call the reef knot), Americans refer to this knot by several other names, including the rustler's knot, the Japanese crown knot, the Japanese success knot, the Chinese cross knot, and the Chinese good luck knot.

1 Make a bight in one of two cords, or one end of a single cord, and pass it around the other cord or end.

2 Lead the second cord up behind the initial bight in the other cord.

3 Bring the second cord down in front of the first one.

4 Pass the first working end over the front of the second to make a locking tuck through the open bight. Flatten and tighten this knot by pulling a bit at a time on each of the four strands that emerge from the knot.

Knife Lanyard Knot

Use this neat little knot to make a cord loop for a tool or to suspend an amulet or ornamental item from a necklace. It is a good-looking, versatile knot with a nautical pedigree.

1 Middle a length of cord, make a bight in one part of it and add a half-twist, as shown, to form a loop.

2 Lay the other part of the cord over the loop in the first part (in the direction shown).

3 Pass the second working end under the original standing part.

4 Then create a locking tuck that goes anticlockwise (counterclockwise) over-under-over-under to create a carrick bend with ends emerging on opposite sides of the knot.

5 Bring the upper, righthand end around anticlockwise (counter-clockwise), over the standing part of the lefthand cord (under everything else) to tuck up through the centre opening.

6 Lead the bottom lefthand working end, similarly, anticlockwise (counterclockwise) over the standing part – but under everything else – to tuck up through the centre panel of the knot. Draw up with the utmost care, removing the slack a bit at a time, and ensuring that both standing parts go down together, while the working ends come up together.

Chinese Lanyard Knot

Less difficult to tie than it appears at first glance, the unusual square shape and texture of this knot make the result worth the effort. It can be used as a decorative means of holding two pieces of cord together – ideal for a necklace. Chinese knotting writer Lydia Chen calls this the plafond knot (*plafond* meaning decorated ceiling) because it resembles the motifs seen in Chinese temples and palaces.

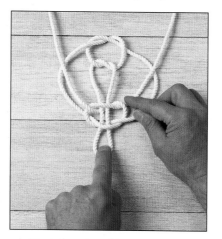

1 Middle a length of cord and make a narrow bight in it.

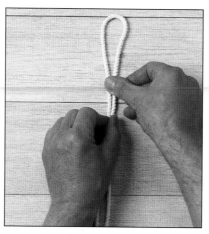

2 Tie a half-knot with both ends of the cord length.

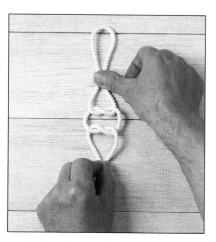

3 Tie an identical second half-knot to complete a loose granny knot.

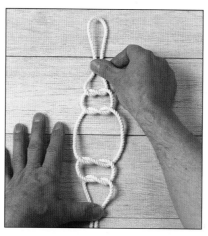

4 Leave a gap of 7–8 cm/about 3 in and tie a second identical granny knot.

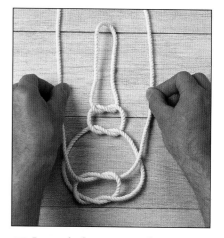

5 Invert the lower granny knot, turning it bottom-for-top.

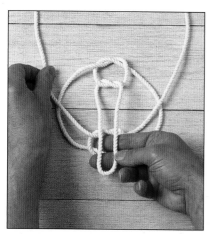

6 Similarly invert the top granny knot, turning it top-for-bottom.

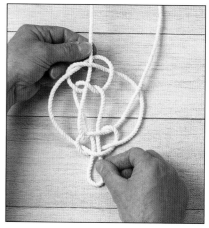

7 Tuck the original bight down through the centre of the lower granny knot.

8 Tuck the lefthand one of the two working ends up through the centre of the upper granny knot.

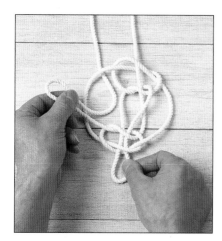

9 Turn the almost completed knot face down and bring the new lefthand working end out to the front.

10 Finally, tuck the lefthand working end up through the upper granny knot. Ensure that the loop is long enough to go over the object it will hold, then patiently remove the slack from this knot (slowly does it), working towards both working ends.

Good Luck Knot

For a robust knot, easy to tie and tighten, this has a striking finished appearance. Use it for gift-wrapped parcels or simply hang it from a belt as a novel chatelaine for keys (keychain). The appearance of this knot will be enhanced if, between the three large loops, the four small ones are left open.

1 Middle a single length of cord and make a narrow bight in it.

2 Pull out and retain a second bight in the lefthand leg of the cord.

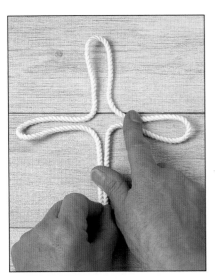

3 Pull out a matching bight in the righthand leg of the cord.

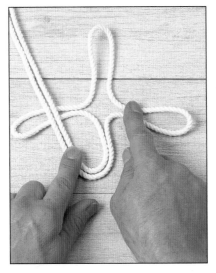

4 Lay both standing parts of the cord up and over the lefthand bight.

5 Take the lefthand bight and lay it over the upper bight.

6 Take the upper bight and lay it down over the righthand bight.

7 Tuck the righthand bight over and through beneath the two standing parts of the cord.

8 Without distorting it in any way, carefully tighten the resulting four-part crown knot.

9 Bring the lefthand bight down and cross the lower bight up over it.

10 Lay the righthand bight up and over the lower bight.

11 Lead the two standing parts of the cord down in a final locking tuck through the vacant bight. Tighten the second crown knot atop the first one.

Chinese Button Knot

This is a classic button knot that can be stitched to a bag or purse and serves either as an attractive fastening or a decorative accessory. Knotted buttons tend to be too large for buttonholes, so fasten them with cord loops or frogs. Tied with craft and patience in very small fine material, button knots make unusual earrings. In some stiff materials, this knot can be made to stay flat, for ornamentation rather than practicality.

1 Middle – more or less – a short length of decorative cord.

2 With one end of the cord make an overhand loop.

3 Then pass the working end down behind the loop just formed.

4 Pick up the other end and tuck it (in this instance, from left to right) under-over-under-over; keep hold of the partially formed knot, as this is not a locking tuck.

5 Finally lead the later working end up and down through the knot as shown.

Prise up as knot tightens

6 Arrange the four-lobed symmetrical knot with the two standing cord parts as a stem, then gradually remove the slack until the knot becomes convex like a mushroom. As it tightens, the central knot part (indicated in the illustration) will tend to recede from sight and must be prised up to the surface of the knot where it will then remain.

Chinese Button Knot (Doubled)

The Chinese button knot is often doubled to produce a bulkier and therefore showier knot. When making this version, it is not necessary to prise up the top central part, which is supported by underlying strands.

1 Continue from step 6 of the Chinese button knot and bring the two working ends alongside one another.

2 Begin to follow the original lead with one of them.

3 Using the other end, start to follow the original lead around in the opposite direction.

4 Continue with both ends until the single-ply knot is entirely doubled.

5 Tuck the ends down through the centre of the knot and carefully tighten it.

Wrapped & Reef Knotted Coil

Rope coiled this way and secured with reef (square) knots has a good chance of surviving any journey tangle-free. This is a quick and simple arrangement that serves to prevent all sorts of frustrating entanglements. It works for thick rope and smaller cordage, and is easy to untie when the rope is required.

1 Bring the two ends of the coiled rope close together, and tie a half-knot (with longer ends than are illustrated).

2 Then add a second half-knot (of opposite handedness) to complete a reef (square) knot.

3 Wrap both ends away from the reef (square) knot, with identical helixes, so as to secure the coil.

4 Where the two ends meet opposite the original reef (square) knot, tie another half-knot.

5 Then add a second half-knot (of opposite handedness) to complete a second reef (square) knot.

Alpine Coil

This is the method of securing a coil of rope for transport that is traditionally preferred by climbers and cavers.

1 Bring the two ends of the coiled rope close together.

2 Bend one end back to create a bight about 15–20 cm/6–8 in long.

3 Wrap the other end around the coiled rope, including the bight.

4 Ensure that the second wrapping turn traps and holds the initial turn.

5 Wrap fairly tightly and keep each succeeding turn snug.

6 Complete at least six wrapping turns, then tuck the working end through the bight (pulling upon the other end to secure it).

Figure-of-Eight Coil

This is the storekeeper's way of hanging coils up out of harm's way. Coiling the rope double is the trick that makes this coil fast and effective, with a practical loop to hang it by. Ropes travelling in the back of a car can always be coiled this way as they can be held in place by securing the loop around a fixed object. It is, like many of the coils, quick and easy to untie, if required in an emergency.

1 Middle the rope prior to coiling and then coil it doubled.

2 Bring the bight back upon itself so as to create a loop.

3 Lead the working bight around the back of the coil to the other side.

4 Finally tuck it up through its own loop (and the entire coil), from front to back, to make a loop from which to hang it.

Fireman's Coil

This method of forming a coil with a useful hanging loop is probably the most basic coil and deserves to be better known.

1 Bring the two ends of the coiled rope close together.

2 With one of the ends, make an overhand small loop.

3 Pass the working end through the coil and behind it, and make a bight.

4 Tuck the bight up through the loop, from behind, and gently pull it tight. Suspend the coil from this loop.

BINDINGS

"I might give up my life for my friend, but he had better not ask me to do up a parcel."
(Logan Pearsall Smith, 1865-1946)

There are two kinds of binding knot. The first is around an object with a wide diameter, where a cord, strap or fabric is wound one or more times and the two ends are then securely tied together (for example, packing parcels, securing a cloth covering to a homemade jar of preserves or applying a first aid tourniquet). The second is for narrow diameters, when a special constricting knot is applied to grip and hold with its own internal friction (for example, to prevent the cut end of a rope from fraying or to attach a hose to a tap). Bindings such as Turk's heads, so named because of their superficial resemblance to turbans, are also ornamental. The Turk's head family is a massive one. Comprehensive books have been written about its various relatives, and some avid knot tyers devote their energy to tracing and becoming familiar with the various types. If the Turk's heads included in this section appeal to you, then their numerous cleverer offspring wait to welcome you elsewhere.

Granny Knot

This is the commonest of knots. Everyone knows how to tie it, but there is little good to be said for it. It either slips or jams and so is totally unreliable; tied as the double granny bow with twin drawloops, it causes shoe-laces to come undone. It is included here solely to highlight its shortcomings, and thus to compare and contrast it with the reef (square), thief and grief knots.

1 Present two ends of the same cord to one another – in this instance, left over right.

2 Tie a half-knot, noting how the two entwined parts spiral to the left, that is, anticlockwise (counterclockwise).

3 Bring the two working ends together, once again left over right.

4 Tie a second half-knot in which the two entwined parts spiral clockwise (or lefthanded).

Reef Knot (Square Knot)

This flat and symmetrical knot of two interlocked bights was known to the ancient Egyptians, Greeks and Romans. With twin drawloops, it becomes the double reef (square) bow, a more secure way to tie shoe-laces. It is strictly a binding knot, reliable only when pressed against something else and tied in both ends of the same material, so restrict its use to bandages and all sorts of parcels (including reefing the sails of small craft).

NOTE – Never use it as a bend.

1 Bring two ends of the same cord together, in this case left over right.

2 Tie a half-knot and see how the two entwined knot parts spiral to the left, anticlockwise (counterclockwise).

3 Bring the two ends back together, but this time right over left.

4 Tie a second half-knot. Note that the two entwined parts helix to the right, anticlockwise (counterclockwise), the opposite of the first half-knot.

Thief Knot

At first glance this looks just like a reef (square) knot – but there is a drastic difference. The short ends are on opposite sides which, of course, cause it to slip and slide due to the uneven pull that this exerts. This renders the knot practically useless in its present form, except as a stepping stone on the way to the robust tumbling thief knot, but it makes a useful teaching aid to quiz those who think they know their knots and their applications.

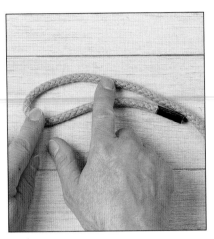

1 Make a small bight in one end of the cord or line.

2 Introduce the other end through the bight just made, angling it towards the short end of the bight.

3 Lead the working end around the back of both parts of the bight.

4 Finally, tuck the working end back through the bight to emerge alongside its own standing part.

Grief Knot

Combining the characteristic failings of both granny and thief knots, this is the most insecure of knots, diagonally unbalanced and with an uneven pull from short ends on opposite sides. But there is a trick to it. Pull both ends and gently roll the knot to tighten it; then lever them on to opposite sides so that they lock solid. In this way the knot can be used to bind together garden trelliswork and similar lightweight structures.

1 Make a small bight in one end of the cord or line.

2 Tuck the working end up through the bight, angling it towards the other short end.

3 Now tuck the working end under the first part of the bight but then over the standing part of the bight.

4 Finally, return the working end back through the bight to emerge from the completed knot alongside its own standing part.

Pole Lashing

A pair of these lashings, plus a couple of reef (square) knots, will seize and subdue an armful of metal tent-poles or any awkward assortment of long and thin objects.

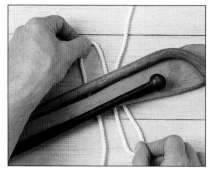

1 Arrange the cord in an "S" or "Z" shape beneath and close to one end of the objects to be tied up.

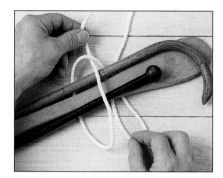

2 Tuck one end down through the bight on the opposite side to it.

3 Bring the other end across and tuck it in its turn down through the remaining bight.

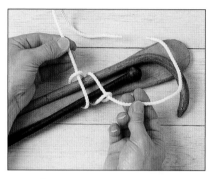

4 Pull up both working ends, so that the bights snugly embrace the enclosed objects.

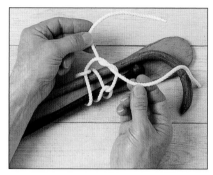

5 Cross the two ends (left over right in this instance), tying the first half of a reef (square) knot, and pulling it tight.

6 Bring the ends back together (right over left) and complete the reef (square) knot. With a second length of cord, repeat steps 1 to 6 at the other end of the objects.

Bag Knot

Like other such knots – which also go under the generic name of sack knots – this dates from the days when grain and other granular or powdered materials were bagged up in sacks, the necks of which were then tied with practised familiarity by millers and grain merchants. Leave a drawloop (as shown) for easy release later if necessary.

1 Wrap the working end of a short length of cord around the neck of the bag or sack.

2 Bring the end up to the left, crossing over itself in the process.

3 Lead the end down behind the bag and then up at the front.

4 Now take the working end across to the right once more, and double it to make a small bight.

5 Finally, tuck the bight to serve as a drawloop, working the completed knot snug and tight.

Sack/Miller's Knot

Unlike the bag knot, the sack knot, which is a binding from an earlier age, cannot be tied in the bight, but it is another one in which a drawloop may be left to prevent possible damage to the bag if the knot is cut.

1 Drape a short length of cord around the neck of the bag or sack with the short end hanging down in front of the bag.

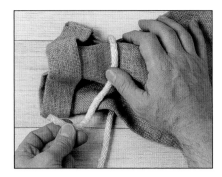

2 Move the short end at the front over to the left.

3 Wrap the longer working end up and over the neck of the bag or sack, from front to back, taking care to trap the short end in place.

4 Take the working end down around the back of the bag and bring it up at the front again.

5 Tuck the end down through the space retained between the first and second wrapping turns and pull it snug and tight. Leave a drawloop, if preferred.

Constrictor Knot, Tied with an End

An alternative to the strangle knot, the constrictor knot can be the best of binding knots. Use it with or without a drawloop as a semi-permanent seizing on rope's ends, hose-pipes, and for every odd job imaginable. The ancient Greeks may have used it for surgical slings, and it could well be the "gunner's knot" that in later centuries seized the necks of flannel-bag gunpowder cartridges for muzzle-loading artillery. It was re-discovered and popularized by Clifford Ashley in 1944. Use this tying method when the end of the foundation rope, spar or whatever, is not easily accessible. To remove a constrictor – without nicking or scarring whatever lies beneath it – carefully sever the overriding diagonal with a sharp knife, when the knot will drop off in two curly cut segments.

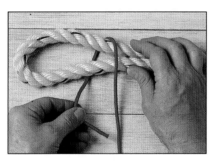

1 Take a short length of cord or twine (hard-laid to bind softer objects, such as rope; soft and stretchy for unyielding foundations) and arrange it around whatever is to be tied.

2 Bring the working end of the binding cord up and across to the right over its own standing part.

3 Lead the end down at the back and up once more at the front.

4 Tuck the working end beneath the diagonal made earlier, completing a clove hitch.

5 Locate and loosen the upper lefthand knot part, preparatory to tucking in the working end.

6 Bring the working end across and tuck it from left to right through the loosened bight. Pull both ends in opposite directions to tighten this knot as hard as possible, when the ends may be cut off quite close to the knot.

Constrictor Knot, Tied in the Bight

This is another example of the excellent constrictor knot. Tie it more quickly this way when the end of the foundation rope, spar, or whatever, is accessible. When pulled tight it will lock securely. With practice, a constrictor knot tied by this method can be applied quicker than the eye can follow the actions.

1 Lead the working end of a short length of cord or twine, from front to back, over the object to be seized.

2 Lift the working end so as to complete a full turn.

3 Pull a fairly long bight down from the lower part of the turn just made.

4 Lift the bight and half-twist it (as shown) to place it over the end of the foundation.

5 Heave on both ends, as strongly as the cord or twine will withstand, to tighten the knot; then cut off the ends close to the knot.

160

Transom Knot

Clifford Ashley originally made this knot to seize together two cross-sticks for his daughter's kite. It is an adaptation of the constrictor knot and can be used for any light trelliswork. If greater strength is needed, add a second knot facing the first one and at right angles to it.

1 The components to be lashed with this knot need to be at right angles.

2 Lead the working end over the horizontal uppermost element of the construction and around the back of the vertical piece.

3 Bring the end diagonally down and across over its own standing part.

4 Now lead it around the back of the vertical piece beneath the horizonal section and return it to the front of the work once more.

5 Tuck the end through beneath the diagonal knot part, so as to form a half-knot with the two opposing cord ends. Pull as tight as possible.

Double Constrictor Knot

This variation of the constrictor knot has extra internal friction and grip; it is also more suitable for binding objects with a larger diameter, or when the objects are an awkward shape and will not automatically pull together. When tying a particularly awkward package and hands are not enough to tighten this seizing as much as required, attach each end of the cord to a screwdriver or similar handle by means of a pile hitch to apply extra leverage.

1 Wrap the cord around the item to be secured. Bring the working end diagonally up and take it across over its own standing part.

2 Lead the working end down behind the work and then up in front once more, taking care to keep between the standing part and the initial turn.

3 Take the working end up and around the foundation again, doubling the characteristic diagonal that overlays the single version of this knot.

4 Put the working end directly down behind, to emerge at the front (on the righthand side of its standing part).

5 Tuck the end through the two turns so it is parallel and to the right of its own standing part.

6 Locate and loosen the upper lefthand part of this almost completed knot, preparatory to the final tuck.

7 Bring the working end across and tuck it from left to right through the loosened bight.

8 Pull the knot as tight as possible and cut the ends off close to the knot.

Boa Knot

This robust binding was devised and announced in 1996 by the accomplished weaver Peter Collingwood, who wanted a knot that would remain securely in place when the foundation around which it was tied was cut close alongside the knot. It combines the structures and qualities of both strangle and double constrictor knots, a really secure arrangement; yet it is quick and easy to tie, and this has ensured its prompt adoption by many discerning knot tyers.

1 Make an overhand loop with a short length of the chosen material.

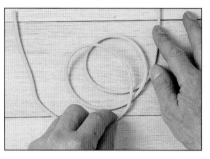

2 Add a similar second turn on top of the first one.

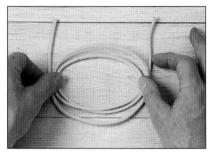

3 Arrange these turns in the form of a coil with both ends lying in the same direction; there should be three cord parts under each thumb.

4 Rotate the righthand side of this coil through 180°, as shown (that is, to put the bottom where the top had been).

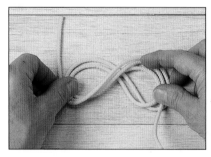

5 Check that the resulting figure-of-eight has three knot parts around each loop and in the overlaying diagonal, with just two parts underneath.

6 Begin to insert the rope, rod or whatever is to be seized, beneath one or other of the end loops.

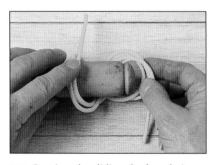

7 Continue by sliding the foundation over the centre crossing, which totals five knot parts.

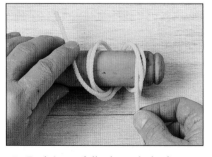

8 Push it carefully through the far loop, when the knot will be completely held upon it.

9 Finally, work this knot snugly into shape, with three twined knot parts overlaid by a pair of diagonals. The ends may be cut much shorter than shown.

Jug, Jar or Bottle Sling

The interwoven knot parts of this clever contrivance will cling unyieldingly to the narrow neck of a bottle, providing it has a very slight, narrow lip, or provide substantial carrying handles for a larger jug or jar (pitcher) – even an ancient Greek amphora. Use it to cool picnic wine in a mountain stream, to lug a churn of milk across the farmyard or to suspend a hanging basket of flowers from a kitchen beam.

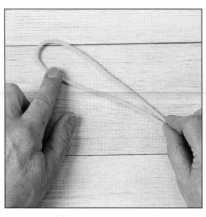

1 Roughly middle an appropriate length of strong cord and make a long bight.

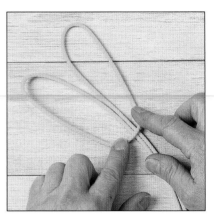

2 Bend the bight down to create two matching long loops.

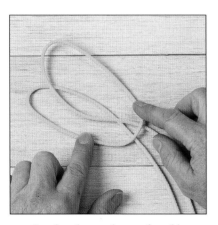

3 Overlap the two loops of cord by laying the righthand one upon the lefthand one.

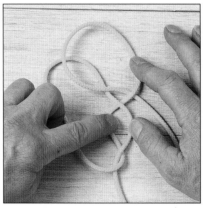

4 Locate the section of cord that overlays both legs of the original bight and begin to pull it up beneath the existing layout.

5 Pull out a bight and make a locking tuck with it over-and-under through the overlapped loops.

6 Extend the working bight about 7 cm/2¾ in beyond the half-completed knot.

7 Take hold of the large curving loop at the back of the knot.

8 Then pull it down to touch the two standing parts of the cord.

9 Take hold of the similar large curving loop at the front of the knot.

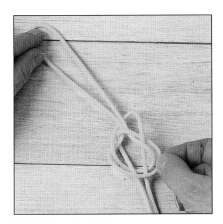

10 Pull this loop down too until it touches the two standing parts of the cord.

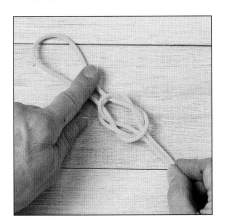

11 Tug gently and experimentally on both bight and cord legs until the tension is evenly distributed throughout the resulting braided bracelet of a knot.

12 Place the knot around the neck of the chosen jug (pitcher), jar or bottle and pull the outer loops as tight as possible.

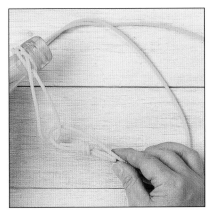

13 Insert one of the long ends through the shorter loop, then tie the two ends together with a fisherman's knot or other secure bend, to create two self-adjusting handles that will always be the same length when held.

Asher's Equalizer

This cunning knot, added to a
jug (pitcher), jar or bottle sling,
adjusts loop lengths automatically
to give two handles the same size,
which makes carrying the object
much easier. It was devised by
Harry Asher in the mid-1980s.

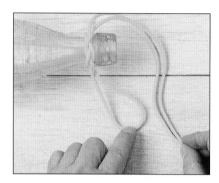

1 Ensure the completed jug (pitcher),
jar or bottle sling has two long ends
and a shorter loop.

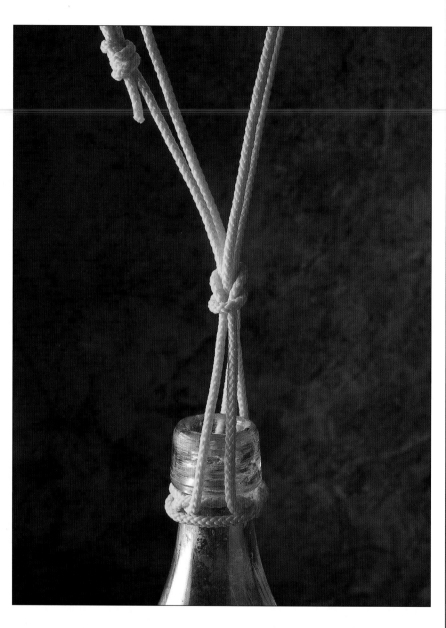

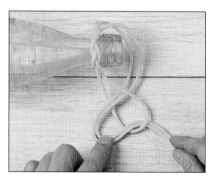

2 Start to pull the two long ends a
short way through the loop until
they create twin bights.

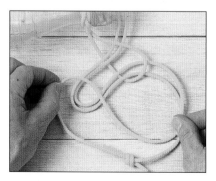

3 Bring the single large loop formed by
the knotted ends over the twin
bights just formed.

4 Pull the twin bights completely
through the single large loop.

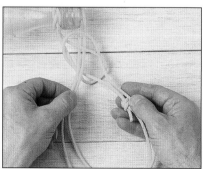

5 Tighten the resulting knot to create
a pair of matching handles.

Double Figure-of-Eight Hitch

Owen K. Nuttall came across this knot as a forerunner to his snuggle hitch; but it is arguably an even better binding knot. The attraction of this particular form is the easily acquired and memorized double figure-of-eight layout. Try it as an alternative to the boa and constrictor knots.

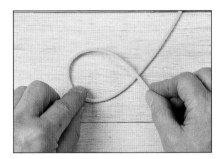

1 First make a clockwise overhand loop with one end of a length of cord or twine.

2 Add an anticlockwise (counterclockwise) overhand loop to form a figure-of-eight.

3 Lay a second clockwise overhand loop on top of the first one.

4 Pick up the other end and place another clockwise overhand loop atop the remaining single loop.

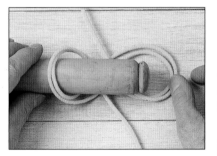

5 Begin to slide the knot over its intended core, or insert the core through the knot, as shown.

6 Locate the knot where required on and around the object to be seized.

7 Pull on both ends as hard as possible to tighten this binding knot.

Square Turk's Head (4 Lead x 5 Bight)

This Turk's head knot has four interwoven strands (or leads) with five scallop-shaped rim parts (bights). These dimensions give it a shorthand label: it is known as a 4-lead x 5-bight Turk's head (abbreviated further when written to 4L x 5B TH). All Turk's heads that have just one lead more or less than the number of bights are also referred to as "square" Turk's heads. This tying method was developed by Charlie Smith.

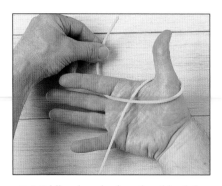

1 Middle a length of cord and lead the working end around the base of the thumb, over the standing part, to go (from front to back) between the first and second fingers.

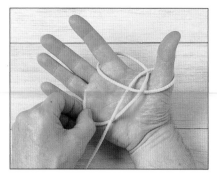

2 Take the end around the forefinger, then up through (under-and-over) the thumb loop, and beneath the standing part.

3 Now lead the working end between the second and third fingers, and around the second finger, to tuck under one/over two/under one (as illustrated).

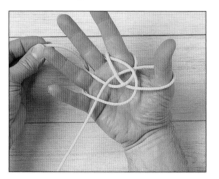

4 Pass the end over the standing part and between the third and little fingers, returning between the second and third fingers and tucking up through the second finger loop.

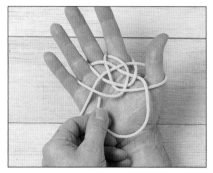

5 Lead the working end, in a final satisfactory locking tuck, over/under/over/under/over, and then tuck the end up alongside the standing part, as shown.

6 The completed knot may remain flattened, or be turned into a bracelet, and (in form) doubled or tripled by following the original lead around with the surplus cord of the unused standing end. The main picture shows a tripled bracelet.

Square Turk's Head (5 Lead x 4 Bight)

Use this single-strand Turk's head instead of one or other of the common whippings to seize the cut ends of ropes. A square Turk's head like this makes a pretty but practical sliding sleeve for the drawcord on a duffel bag. Then again, it can embellish anything it will fit, from bellropes and handrails to key fobs or the gear shift of a classic sports car.

1 Middle a length of cord and pass the working end over and down behind the core, to reappear on the right of the standing part. Go diagonally up (from right to left) over the previous lead.

2 Take the end over, around and down behind the core, emerging to the immediate right of the standing part, tucking over one/under one/ over one, from right to left.

3 Lead the working end down behind the core, to reappear again just to the right of the standing part, and tuck (left to right) under one/over one.

4 Rotate the work, bringing the rear side into view, and tuck the end (right to left) over/under/over.

5 Turn the work back to its original position and tuck the working end to the right of the standing part (and left to right) over/under/over.

6 Rotate the work, to show the rear side. Lead the end (right to left) in a final locking tuck under/over/under/over.

7 Place the working end alongside the standing part to complete the knot, which may then be doubled and tripled by following around the original lead with the surplus cord.

Twined Turk's Head (2 Lead x 3 Bight)

This primitive version of a Turk's head is unusual. It is rarely seen, although it has been used to bind the ends of hunting crops.

1 Tie an overhand knot around the chosen core with the working end of a length of cord.

2 Lead the end over, around and down behind the core, to reappear to the right of the standing part.

3 Tuck the working end alongside the standing part and parallel to it.

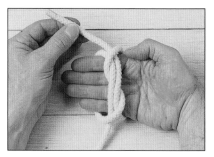

4 Follow the original lead with the working end, tucking under and staying parallel to it (on the same side).

5 Continue to reproduce the original lead, doubling the knot with the working end.

6 Tuck the working end under the next loop, following the standing part as before.

7 Tuck the working end in to complete. Make a 2L x 3B TH this way. With an initial double overhand knot, produce a 2L x 5B TH. A treble overhand knot results in a 2L x 7B TH. A quadruple overhand knot creates a 2L x 9B TH, and so on.

Spade End Knot

Anglers attach monofilament to spade-ended (eyeless) hooks, or short leader lengths to thicker lines, with this knot. It is akin to perfected whipping.

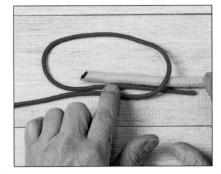

1 Make a loop in the thinner stuff and arrange it so that the short end is alongside the thicker line.

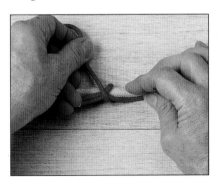

2 Leaving the short end in position, begin to wrap the body of the loop, enclosing and holding both parts of itself as well as the thicker line.

3 Continue to bind tightly, with each succeeding turn snugly up against the preceding one.

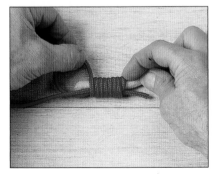

4 Complete about 2 cm/¾ in of wrapping, then pass the shrunken loop over the end of the thicker line.

5 Remove any remaining slack from the bight, then pull in opposite directions on both ends to tighten.

LOOPS

*"A hemp noose rough on the sunburned skin
of the neck . . ."*
(DOUGLAS BOTTING – *THE PIRATES*, 1979)

The hangman's noose, brandished by every
Hollywood lynch mob, is a splendid example
of a secure and strong knot designed to absorb
a shock loading without breaking the rope. It
is just one of the family of blood or barrel-
shaped knots, with several wrapping turns,
utitilized in their own specialized materials by
anglers, cavers and climbers, veterinarians and
surgeons – but not, in fact, by many public
executioners. They preferred a simple
reinforced eye with the standing part of the
rope passing freely through it. A loop knot may
be used like a hitch, but placed over a post or
rail (rather than tied around it), the advantage
being that it is easily removed again for re-use.
Double and multiple loops are for improvised
working hoists and rescue slings (in the absence
of better alternatives). Running knots or
nooses, useful for parcels, may have originated
as snares to catch animals and birds for food.
Some loops are tied in the bight, others in the
end of cordage.

CAUTION
A growing body of legislation discourages the use of makeshift
loop knots, and improvised slings, in favour of properly
manufactured and tested safety harnesses and rigging.
Nevertheless, there will always be situations when – to save life
– it might still be acceptable to grab a coil of rope and put
together a rescue knot or two. At those times, one or other of
the following knots would still be justified.

Angler's Loop

This is an old angling knot, from the 17th-century days of Sir Izaak Walton and lines made of gut, which has resurfaced as a secure loop knot for the latest manmade ropes. It will even stay tied in bungee (elasticated) shock cord. This knot too can be tied in the bight, but the method illustrated is easier to learn and remember.

1 Immobilize the end of the line and make an overhand loop with the standing part.

2 Bring the end over and lay it across the initial loop.

3 Pull a bight through to create what is, at this stage, an overhand knot with a drawloop.

4 Lead the working end around behind the standing part of the line.

5 Tuck the end through the centre of the knot, trapping it neatly beneath the two legs of the loop.

Figure-of-Eight Loop

Referred to by sailormen once upon a time as a Flemish loop, the figure-of-eight loop was viewed by them with disfavour because it tended to jam in wet hemp or manilla ropes and could not easily be untied after loading. Cavers and climbers now prefer this versatile alternative to the bowline. It is easily tied – even by an uncertain beginner – and readily checked by a team leader (in the poorest light and the worst weather). Tie the working end to the standing part for added security.

1 Make a generous bight in the end of the cord or rope.

2 Impart half a twist in the bight to create twin loops, as shown.

3 Add an extra half-twist to the loops already produced, as shown.

4 Tuck the bight through the twin loops and work the completed knot neatly snug and tight.

Bowline

Once this knot was used for attaching a line from the bow of a ship to the weather leech of a square-sail, holding it closer to the wind, and thus preventing it being taken aback (blown inside out). Nowadays the same bowline (pronounced "boh-linn") is used, misused and abused for innumerable other jobs from tying parcels to tree surgery. Among its advantages are that it does not slip, loosen or jam. It remains a time-honoured knot, which may, however, need to have its working end tied or taped to the adjacent loop leg for added security.

1 Bring the working end across the standing part of the rope to form an overhand loop.

2 Rotate the hand clockwise and so produce a smaller loop in the standing part of the rope.

3 Ensure that the working end points upwards (from back to front) through the small loop.

4 Lead the end around behind the standing part of the rope.

5 Then tuck it back down through the small loop, this time from front to back.

6 Arrange the completed knot with a long end (longer than shown) and consider further securing it with tape, a half hitch or other extra fastening.

Eskimo Bowline

This variation on the orthodox bowline is sometimes referred to as the Boas bowline. The Arctic explorer Sir John Ross (1777–1856) brought an Inuit (Eskimo) sled back to England that had been presented to him by Inuits. It contained numerous such knots in its rawhide lashings, evidence that this was a genuine Inuit knot. The sled is now in the basement of the Museum of Mankind, London. As it is more secure than the common bowline, especially in synthetic lines, it is worth learning.

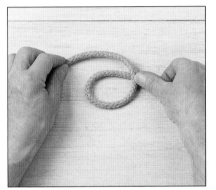

1 Make an underhand loop in one end of the rope.

2 Bring the standing end down behind the loop, creating an incomplete overhand knot.

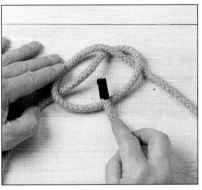

3 Lift the standing part of the rope up slightly within the loop.

4 Then make a locking tuck (over/under/over) with the working end of the rope.

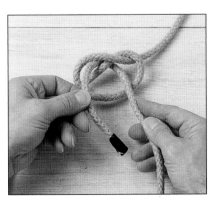

5 Let the working end be pulled into a bight by the marlinespike hitch.

6 Draw the marlinespike hitch down over the bight. Note the untypical face of this bowline, when tightened, with its distinctive trefoil crown.

Double Bowline

With the reinforced nip, this knot is stronger (70 to 75 per cent) and more secure than the common bowline. With a fairly long end, it may not need to be taped or tied.

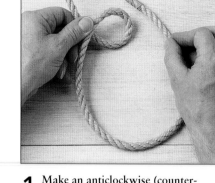

1 Make an anticlockwise (counter-clockwise) overhand loop.

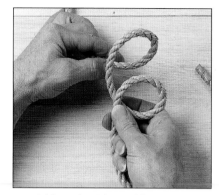

2 Add another identical loop above (or behind) the first one.

3 Bring the two loops together, preparatory to tucking the working end through them.

4 Tuck the end up through the combined loops from behind.

5 Lead the working end around behind the standing part of the rope.

6 Then tuck it down through the double loop, beside its own other part, with a moderately long tail end.

Water Bowline

It is claimed that this version of the common bowline is less liable to jam when wet (hence its name). This is certainly one of the more secure bowlines, and it withstands rougher handling and dragging over rugged terrain.

1 Form the loop that is typical of most sorts of bowline.

2 Make a loop of the required size and tuck the working end up through the loop from behind.

3 Add a second loop, in the standing part, identical to the first one.

4 Pass the working end up through this second loop as well.

5 Take the working end around the back of the standing part.

6 Then tuck it down beside its own standing part through both the upper and lower loops. Tighten the basic bowline, and then pull the lower loop up snug alongside that knot.

Blood Loop Dropper Knot

Tied in angling lines, this knot makes a strong starting loop for a paternoster tackle system, although some anglers argue that it should be limited to fly-fishing. In the much thicker cord illustrated here, it forms a useful loop in the middle of a line for all kinds of attachments.

1 Form a loop as the starting point for a triple overhand knot.

2 Tie a simple overhand knot, keeping the loop looser than illustrated.

3 Take a second tuck with one or other of the working ends.

4 Now take a third tuck to arrive at a triple overhand knot.

5 Locate the centre of the two twined knot parts and then pull the original single loop down between the two knot parts into a small bight.

6 Carefully shape and work the knot snug and tight, with the loop at the required size.

Farmer's Loop

This solid little knot continues to appeal to knot tyers because of its leapfrog method of tying. It acquired its name when Professor Howard W. Riley included it in his 1912 pamphlet as a knot used on American farms.

1 Wrap a complete turn around the hand from the back to the front.

2 Add a further turn, so that there are now three cord parts on both sides of the hand.

3 Shift the middle turn up and over, so that it becomes the righthand part.

4 Raise the newly created middle knot part and carry this over to the left.

5 Take the latest centre knot part and transfer it to the outer right position.

6 Locate and pull up what is now the centre part; this will be the loop of this knot's name.

7 With a loop of the required size, carefully tighten the knot.

Manharness Knot

This is an ancient knot, although as recently as 1992 American Mike Storch recommended a series of these knots spaced out along a picket line to tether horses. It is tied in the bight.

1 Make an anticlockwise (counterclockwise) overhand loop.

2 Bring the upper section of line around to the back of the loop.

3 Press the righthand side of the original loop to the left beneath the middle (rearward) knot part.

4 Then pull it further left, over the lefthand side of the loop.

5 Hold onto the loop and pull the knot to tighten it.

Alpine Butterfly

This is a European mountaineering classic middleman's tie-on. If, as A.P. Herbert (1890–1971) wrote in a poem, "the bowline is the king of knots", then the Alpine butterfly, added Scouting's ropework writer John Sweet, must surely be the queen. Its other name, given to it by Clifford Ashley, is the lineman's loop. It is tied in the bight.

1 Lay a bight of rope over one hand at the point where the knot is required.

2 Lead the working part of the rope around the hand a second time to complete one round turn.

3 Add a third turn with the rope around the hand.

4 Pick up the righthand turn and relocate it between the other two turns.

5 Pick up the new righthand turn and leap-frog it across to become the lefthand turn.

6 Tuck the lefthand rope part through (from left to right) beneath the other two turns.

7 Pull out a bight of the required size and then pull on both standing parts of the rope to tighten the knot.

185

Three-Quarter Figure-of-Eight Loop

A variation of the basic figure-of-eight loop, this was devised around 1980 by the Canadian rock and building climber Robert Chisnall, who wanted a knot that could be pulled in either direction without distorting it (a demand often made upon such knots). It is relatively new, so try it out in safe situations to discover just how it performs as an alternative to other classic knotted loops such as the alpine butterfly.

1 Make a clockwise underhand loop, then take the working end up behind the loop and bring it forward (over and down) in front of the loop.

2 Tuck the working end from left to right, under and over.

3 Bring the other end of the line around beneath the standing part.

4 Then tuck it over the standing part and down through the knot. Pull the loop first, then the two rope parts, to tighten the knot.

Frost Knot

The Frost knot is just a simple overhand loop that is tied in webbing. This is used in the improvised short lengths of climbing ladders called étriers (French: stirrups). It was devised by Tom Frost some time in the 1960s. This has essentially been created for use as a tape knot, and is not, therefore, generally tied in cordage.

1 Make a short bight in one end of a length of webbing or tape and insert the other end between the two flat sections of the bight.

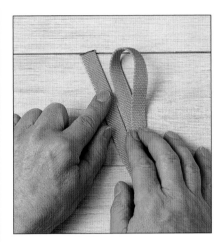

2 Form an anticlockwise (counter-clockwise) overhand loop with all three parts of the webbing or tape.

3 Take the bight and its extra end around behind the loop and pull them through to tie what is in effect a compound overhand knot.

4 Tighten the completed knot, taking care to keep all three sections flat and together.

Double Frost Knot

In combination with the basic Frost knot, this variation of its simple relative improvises the foot loops in étriers (short webbing ladders).

1 Make matching bights in two suitable lengths of climbing webbing.

2 Form one of the two bights into an overhand loop.

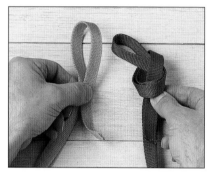

3 Then complete the tying of a simple overhand knot with the bight.

4 Insert the other bight through the knot to lie on top of the first bight.

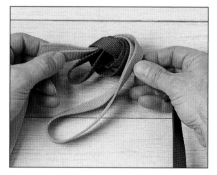

5 Follow the lead of the knotted first bight with the second one.

6 Ensure, as the knot is progressively doubled, that all of the webbing parts lie flat together.

7 Tighten the completed knot, leaving twin loops of the required size.

Double Figure-of-Eight

This double looped version of the climbers' popular basic knot was described in 1944 by Clifford Ashley. It is tied in the bight. A useful characteristic of this particular variation of the original knot is the absence of any ends that might work loose, which helps to make it relatively secure. The twin loops generally tend to emerge the same size. If each one must be a different length, arrange this by patiently feeding slack line as required through the completed knot.

1 Middle the rope as required, form a bight, and with it create a clockwise underhand loop.

2 Bring the end of the bight around (from right to left) in front of the twin standing parts of the rope.

3 Take the bight down behind the loop, and then begin to pull it partially through.

4 Adjust the emerging couple of loops to the required size.

5 Place the end of the bight over the newly formed loops.

6 Then pass the bight over the entire knot to secure the paired loops.

Spanish Bowline

The splayed loops of this ancient knot can hoist a person aloft, or lower them safely, with a leg thrust through each. It is used by fire brigades, coastguards and rescue teams and is also known as the chair knot. However, anyone being lifted would have to hold firmly to the standing parts of the rope at chest level so as not to be tipped out, so re-read the caution at the opening of this section concerning improvised rescue knots. This bowline is a tried and trusted old knot with a maritime background.

1 Middle – or make a long bight in – the rope, doubling it to create two twin loops.

2 Impart an upward, anticlockwise (counterclockwise) half twist to the lefthand loop.

3 Impart a matching upward (but clockwise) mirror-image half twist to the righthand loop.

4 Keeping the previously created twists, pass the lefthand loop through the righthand loop.

5 Rearrange, or allow the rope to open out, to the simple layout shown.

6 Enlarge the lower crossing turn, producing two bights.

7 Lift and half twist both lower loops. Pass them through the upper loops.

8 Pull the two loops outwards until they are the required size; pull down on the standing parts to tighten the knot. If one end is close to the knot, secure it to the adjacent standing part with a double overhand knot.

Brummycham Bowline

Neatest with just two loops, this knot may be tied with many more loops by treating it like a coil of rope. Its name is no doubt derived from the local nickname for the city of Birmingham, "Brum", where the knot's British innovator, Harry Asher, resided.

1 Double one end of a rope to create a bight no longer than the length of the intended loops.

2 Make a loop of the required size with the long end of the rope.

3 Make a second loop of the required size with the long end of the rope (add three or more loops if necessary).

4 Form an underhand loop with the long end of the rope.

5 Pass the loop over the top of the two (or more) bights.

6 Pass the working end through all of the upper bights from back to front to complete this knot.

Triple Figure-of-Eight

This is yet another of those useful climbing contrivances created in the mid-1980s by Canadian Robert Chisnall.

1 Middle – or make a long bight in – the rope to be tied.

2 Make a clockwise underhand loop with the previously made bight.

3 Bring the bight over the twin standing parts from right to left.

4 Lay the working bight behind the original loop (from the left).

5 Then pull twin loops through, at the same time creating a doubled figure-of-eight layout.

6 Adjust the newly formed twin loops to the required length.

7 Finally, lead the bight over the twin standing parts, from left to right, and tuck it (back to front) through beside the existing two loops to form a third one.

Triple Bowline

Robert Chisnall devised this triple bowline; tied in the bight, for training purposes, it enables instructor and pupil to belay to a tree or other anchorage (with a secure loop for each).

1 Middle – or make a long bight in – the climbing rope.

2 Lay the working end of the bight over the standing part.

3 Bend the bight down and tuck it through the twin loops.

4 Pull up the bight, tripping the standing parts into the bowline form.

5 Adjust the twin loops thus formed to the required length.

6 Take the working end around the back of the standing parts.

7 Tuck the bight down (from front to back) through the knot, forming the third loop. Grasp all six loop legs in one hand, holding the two standing parts in the other, and pull apart to tighten. If one of the standing parts is short, tie it to its partner with a double overhand knot.

Bowstring Knot

Limited adjustment makes this knot suitable for small roles such as tightening or slackening tent guy lines or washing lines. It has been used to improvise the sliding loop on American cowboys' lassoes and the lariats of the Spanish vaqueros; while the ancient Briton, Lindow Man – whose 2,000-year-old mummified remains are now displayed in the British Museum, London – was strangled with a similar knot.

1 With the working end of a rope, make a clockwise underhand loop.

2 Tuck the working end through the loop to produce an overhand knot.

3 Take the working end through the end compartment of the overhand knot, ensuring that the over-under sequence is precisely as shown (no other way will do).

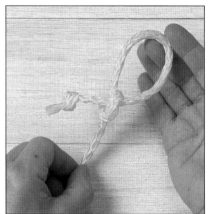

4 Tighten the knot, adding a small stopper knot to prevent the end from pulling free.

Midshipman's Hitch

This is a slide-and-grip knot, which may be grasped and slid by hand to where it is required (after which it holds firm), making it suitable for tensioning guy lines, stays or shrouds. The name implies a Royal Navy origin.

1 Make a clockwise overhand loop of approximately the required size.

2 Bring the working end around and tuck it from the back through the loop just formed.

3 Take the working end up and begin a wrapping turn, which must cross and trap its own earlier turn.

4 Bring the working end once again through the loop and continue to wrap it (towards the standing part).

5 Take the working end up and around the standing part, so that two turns now diagonally overlay and trap the original turn.

6 Lead the working end outside the loop and take it from left to right across the front of the standing part.

7 Finally, create a half hitch around the standing part of the line and tighten it so that it lies alongside the other riding turns.

Tarbuck Knot

This slide-and-grip knot was popularized by Ken Tarbuck for the new-fangled nylon climbing ropes. However, it was already employed by American tree trimmers in 1946, who referred to it simply as "the knot". It relies for its grip upon creating a dog's leg in the standing part of the rope; so it is not, as sometimes suggested, a useful hitch to resist a lateral pull, since a rigid rail or spar will not yield the required deformation. It is now shunned as a climbing knot, because it could rupture and ruin the outer sheath of kernmantel ropes.

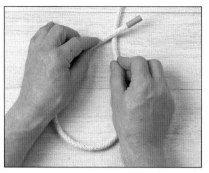

1 Make a loop of roughly the required size for the job in hand.

2 Tuck the working end down and around behind the loop.

3 Bring the end up out of the loop, and begin to perform a second wrapping turn.

4 Wrap around the standing part and down a second time, bringing the end out through the loop.

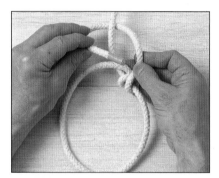

5 Complete two turns around the standing part of the rope, and divert the working end to pass around behind the standing part.

6 Bring back the working end and tuck it through its latest loop from right to left. Tighten the knot, a bit at a time, until all slack has been removed.

Adjustable Loop

Another creation from Canadian climber Robert Chisnall, this loop can easily be shifted by hand in either direction – but it seizes when loaded. A safety feature of this knot (and of all slide-and-grip knots) is that shock loading will cause it to slide until friction reduces the load to a manageable percentage, when it will hold.

1 Make a loop with the working end laid over the standing part.

2 With the working end, take a turn around the standing part.

3 Take a second turn around the standing part with the working end.

4 Now pass the working end around both legs of the loop.

5 Finally, tuck the working end beneath the second wrapping turn.

Hangman's Noose

The grisly name of this knot should not be allowed to detract from its general usefulness. It is – with the exception of the bimini twist – the ultimate strong and secure loop. The snug wrapping turns of this knot are an indication of its shock-absorbing slide-and-grip characteristics. Ensure that when applying the turns you keep them close alongside one another.

1 Form a flattened "S" or "Z" shape in the end of a length of rope or cord.

2 Begin to wrap the twin legs of the loop with the working end.

3 Take care to trap the third cordage part in the groove between the other two parts.

4 Continue to wrap the working end around the three enclosed knot parts, ensuring that all three nest close together in a triangular cross-section.

5 Ensure that each turn is made fairly tight by pulling steadily on the working end.

6 Continue to make wrapping turns with the working end, keeping them snug and tight.

7 Aim to do at least seven turns (sailors' knotlore says that the number seven represents the seven seas).

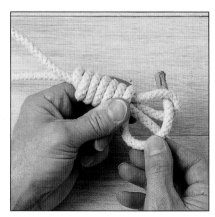

8 Finally, tuck the working end through the nearby small loop and trap it by pulling upon whichever one of the two legs of the large loop closes the other loop.

Arbor Knot

Primarily a knot attaching
monofilament or braid to an
arbor (a reel or spool), this knot
is also used as a shock-absorbing
slide-and-grip knot when securing
a line to a hook or lure.

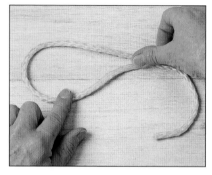

1 Make a bight near to one end of the
monofilament, braid or other line.

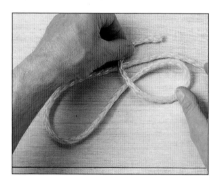

2 Keeping the two parallel line parts
close together, form a small loop by
laying the working end across them.

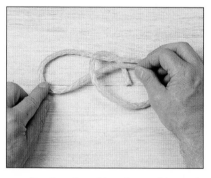

3 Continue by taking the working end
down behind the emerging knot.

4 Bring the end up out of the loop and
complete a round turn of the two
bight parts.

5 Take the working end down behind
the knot once more.

6 Complete a second turn, keeping the
wrappings tight as they are tied.

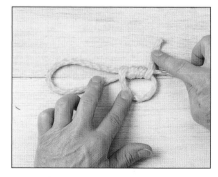

7 Take a third turn with the working
end, ensuring that all are snug
against one another. Tighten the small
loop, and trap the end by pulling on one
of the large loop legs.

Bimini Twist

This remarkably strong loop (95–100 per cent), recommended for big game fishing, has been in print since at least 1975. It is illustrated for clarity in much larger cordage than would in fact be used; consequently, it was not possible to show realistically how the hands – and feet – would actually cooperate in tying this knot with fine monofilament or braid. Still, the various stages are correctly shown. The numerous initial twists, simply imparted with a forefinger, are then spread apart to create the overlaying series of wrapping turns that strengthen and finish off this knot.

1 Make a bight over 50 cm/20 in long. Insert a finger in the end of the bight and begin to twist a loop around.

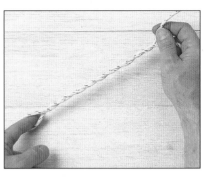

2 Impart some 20 twists to the bight, holding both parts of the line so that they do not unwind.

3 Spread the loop. In practice, this must be done with the feet, while both hands are free to control the two upper ends of the line. Start to enlarge the loop to unwind the initial twists.

4 An overriding layer of wrapping turns should appear where the hands are focused. Hold the standing part taut and feed the working end at right angles into these turns under steady tension, keeping them tight and close together.

5 With the working end, take a half hitch around one leg of the large loop.

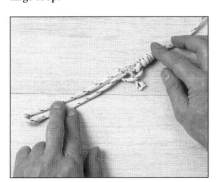

6 Finally, make a half hitch with the working end around both legs of the loop.

Portuguese Bowline

Old-time sailormen were a polyglot tribe who shipped aboard any vessel that would have them, so knot names spread haphazardly. Felix Reisenberg called this a French bowline; whereas Clifford Ashley, who spotted it aboard Portuguese boats in his home town of New Bedford, Massachusetts, gave it the current name. It was used as a kind of boatswain's chair, with the crewman's legs through one loop and his back supported by the other one.

1 Form a small overhand loop with the working end of the rope.

2 Make a large loop in the same direction and of roughly the required working size.

3 As the working end approaches the smaller loop, take it behind.

4 Bring it up and through the cinch as if tying a common bowline.

5 Take the end around the back of the standing part of the rope.

6 Finally, tuck the end down through the cinch and tighten the resulting knot around the two trapped loop parts. Ensure the end is longer than illustrated.

Portuguese Bowline with Splayed Loops

A couple of these versatile knots will sling a plank or ladder as an improvised work platform, but note that each one of the two loops can pull slack from the other. Do not use this knot in circumstances where this may prove an undesirable feature. An illustration of this knot appeared in *Tratado de Apparelho do Navio*, (1896), Lisbon, and Clifford Ashley reports having first seen it used aboard Portuguese ships.

1 Arrange the line as shown in the illustration above.

2 Reduce the size of the lower loop, secure the lefthand bight, and bring the working end around to create a second loop on the righthand side of the emerging knot.

3 Tuck the working end up through the small central loop and then take the end around behind the standing part of the rope.

4 Finally, tuck the end down through the central loop or cinch. Adjust the two working loops to the required size, and then begin to tighten the familiar bowline layout.

Tom Fool's Knot

This is one of many so-called handcuff knots that, according to knot lore, can render any Houdini helpless. In fact, they were probably used for hobbling farm animals overnight, as an alternative to a picket line, so as to leave them free to graze. Tie this knot in the bight.

1 Cast a clockwise overhand loop, tying it in the bight of the chosen rope or cord.

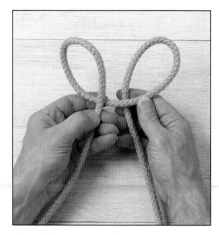

2 Add an anticlockwise (counterclockwise) underhand loop, of similar size to the first one.

3 Partly overlap the two loops, the lefthand one in front of the righthand one, and prepare to pull the leading edge of the lefthand loop (from the front to the back) through the righthand loop, at the same time pulling the leading edge of the righthand loop (from the back to the front) through the lefthand loop.

4 Pull out twin loops, adjust them to the required size, then tighten the knot.

Handcuff Knot

This takes a second or so more to
tie than the simple Tom Fool's
knot since the twin loops are
interlocked, but it is doubtful that
this more elaborate version is
stronger or more stable than the
simpler knot.

1 Cast a clockwise overhand loop,
tying it in the bight of the rope.

2 Add a second loop, anticlockwise
(counterclockwise) and underhand.

3 Partly overlap the loops, with the
righthand one coming in front of the
lefthand one.

4 Pull the leading edge of the lefthand
loop (from the back to the front)
through the righthand loop; at the same
time pull the leading edge of the
righthand loop (from the front to the
back) through the lefthand loop.

5 Adjust the loops to the required size
and then tighten the knot.

Fireman's Chair Knot

Either the handcuff knot or the Tom Fool's knot is the basis for this. Colin Grundy, who studied the fireman's chair knot, reported that either worked well. One loop, adjusted for size, fits beneath the subject's armpits, with the other loop around behind the knees. A rescuer then lowers the person by means of one long end, while a second rescuer pulls them away from the wall, cliff or other hazard with the lower rope.

1 Cast a clockwise overhand loop in the bight of the rescue rope.

2 Then add an anticlockwise (counterclockwise) underhand loop of similar size to the first one.

3 Partly overlap both loops, ensuring that the righthand one is in front of the left.

4 Pull the leading edge of the lefthand loop (from the back to the front) through the righthand loop; at the same time pull the leading edge of the righthand loop (from the front to the back) through the lefthand loop.

5 Pull on both loops at once to tighten the knot so far formed.

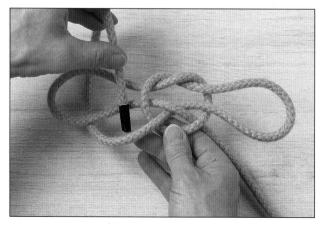

6 Take the lefthand standing part around the back of the lefthand loop and bring it over to the front.

7 Take the working end down through its own loop to tie a half hitch.

8 Take the righthand standing part over the top of the righthand loop and round the back.

9 Tuck the working end through its own loop from back to front to tie another half hitch.

MATS, PLAITS, RINGS, SLINGS & THINGS

"With a bit of string and a modicum of topological ingenuity it was possible to convert my long-sleeved sweater into an impromptu rucksack . . ."
(SIR FRED HOYLE – OSSIAN'S RIDE, 1959)

Knots are like tools. It is possible to muddle along with four or five, using and misusing them for every task imaginable. The best strategy, however, is to acquire a full and varied repertoire of bends, hitches and other contrivances, so that you always have precisely the correct combination for the job in hand. There are many knots, bends and hitches that may be used only infrequently; but, when they are, nothing else will do as well. What follows is a selection of these occasional knots.

Barrel Sling

Use this split form of the overhand knot to hoist or lower an open barrel, cask or drum that is partly full. The working end must be secured to the standing part of the rope, and care must also be taken to ensure that the bottom loop is unable to slip from beneath the load. This sling appears barely adequate for the job, yet it was once a handy favourite with crews shifting cargoes of tubs, casks and barrels.

1 Place the lifting line beneath the load and tie a half knot on top.

2 Split the half knot in two and work each knot part down over the load.

3 Pull both legs of the divided knot snug around the load.

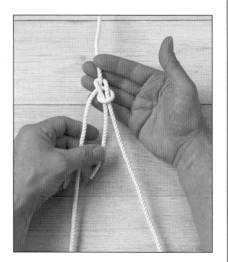

4 Finally, tie a bowline in the shorter end to the standing part.

Plank Sling

A grown-up relative of pole lashings but made with ropes rather than cords. A couple of plank slings will improvise a working platform.

1 Place one end of the rope beneath the plank or other staging.

2 Push an extra bight beneath the plank, making an "S" or "Z" shape.

3 Bring one end of the rope across and tuck it through the bight on the opposite side of the plank.

4 Take the other end across and tuck it through the opposite bight.

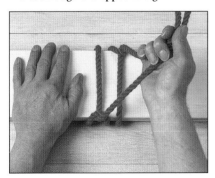

5 Adjust and tighten the sling so that the tips of the bights are just above the edges of the plank, on the working surface; then tie the shorter end to the standing part of the rope.

Jury Mast Knot

With its three adjustable loops, this knot's day job was once to rig a makeshift (jury) mast in a boat. Each of the loops and the two ends made attachment points for the necessary shrouds and stays in order to steady and support it. Nowadays, it is reduced to celebrity appearances as a knot tyer's party piece.

1 Cast a clockwise overhand loop in the bight of the rope.

2 Add an anticlockwise (counterclockwise) underhand loop and partially overlap the two (lefthand loop over righthand).

3 Make another anticlockwise (counterclockwise) underhand loop, to the right of the existing couple, and partially overlap it below the centre loop.

4 Further overlap the lefthand and the righthand loops (the right over the left) within the middle loop.

5 Pull the leading edge of the righthand loop – under/over – to create a long lefthand loop.

6 Pull the leading edge of the lefthand loop over/under to produce a matching righthand loop.

7 Lastly, pull the upper edge of the centre loop up to create an upper third loop.

Three-Way Sheet Bend

For a three-way bridle of converging lines, consider this simple yet effective solution. It was first reported in 1990 by the Swedish marine artist and knotting writer Frank Rosenow, who spotted it while cruising in Greek waters.

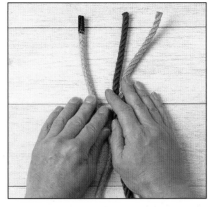

1 Bring together three pieces of rope, which may be of dissimilar size and texture.

2 Make a bight in one of the lines – the larger or stiffer, if there is one.

3 Tuck both of the other lines up through the bight.

4 Wrap the two lines around the bight and tuck them beneath themselves, so that all three working ends are on the same side of the finished knot.

Monkey's Fist

Add weight where it will improve the flight and distance of a messenger or throwing line with this time-honoured knot. It needs a core to retain its shape – something heavy like a round stone, which should be inserted before completing the last three turns. Take care to throw the knotted rope's end within arm's length of the catcher (but not directly at him or her) as the core can make this knot very heavy.

1 Choose a line of appropriate weight and thickness; a line that floats is preferable for use over water.

2 Make three complete turns, working away from the short end, and hold them flat (each one beside the next).

3 Turn the line 90° and add another similar complete turn.

4 Continue to add two more complete turns. Ensure that the second set of turns lies flat and enclose the first three turns.

5 Turn the line 90° again, and tuck the end through at the top of the knot, between the two sets of turns.

6 Then tuck the end through at the bottom of the knot, between the two sets of turns.

7 Complete three final turns, at right angles to the first two sets of turns; insert a round stone, discarded squash ball or other hard filler of the right size, and painstakingly, a bit at a time, tighten all of the wrapping turns. Secure the short end to the standing part of the line with a knot or tape.

Half Hitching

Long parcels of many different shapes and sizes (from carpets to lengths of plastic plumbing from a do-it-yourself store) may be tied with a series of half hitches to secure them. Once you have tied the first binding loop, continue to arrange them so that they are spaced at neat and regular intervals and the pressure on the surface of the parcel is consistent. Apply gentle tension by means of the crossing knots on the return journey.

1 Make a sliding loop around the goods, from a small fixed loop with the long end tucked through it.

2 Cast an underhand loop (clockwise, in this instance), tying it in the bight.

3 Slip the loop over the end of the parcel and pull the resulting half hitch tight.

4 Add a series of such half hitches, tied in the bight, tightening them so that they are aligned and equidistant from one another.

5 Turn the work over, when the end is reached, and – at the first crossing point – tie a crossing knot.

6 Add a series of such crossing knots, tensioning each one so as to retain the spacing of the original half hitches.

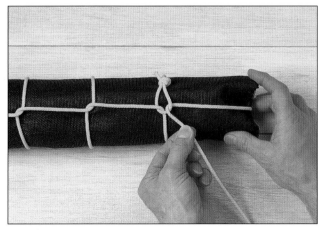

7 Go around the other end of the parcel, and tie off to the original small fixed loop.

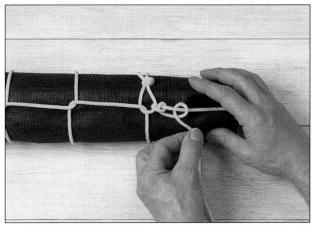

8 Finally, complete the package by tying off with a couple of half hitches.

Marline Hitching

Marline hitching looks identical to half hitching, but it is in fact very different. Try sliding both kinds off: half hitching collapses to nothing, which means that it can be tied in the bight, while marline hitching emerges as a string of overhand knots (and so requires a working end). This method tends to cling better during the tying process, but is somewhat slower to do than the simpler half hitching. Use it to lash up a garden hammock for winter storage or a carpet when moving house, and to parcel any other awkwardly long load.

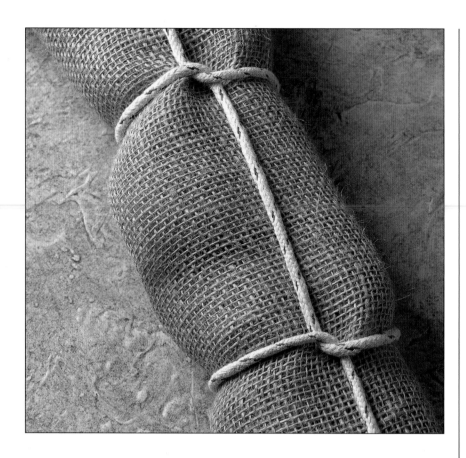

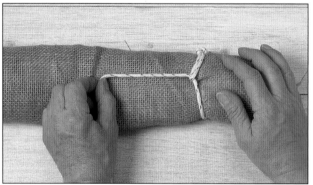

1 Start with a sliding noose around the goods, tied from a small fixed loop with the working end passed through it.

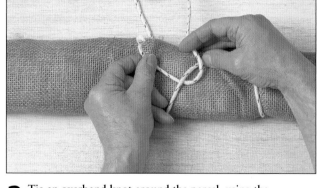

2 Tie an overhand knot around the parcel, using the working end.

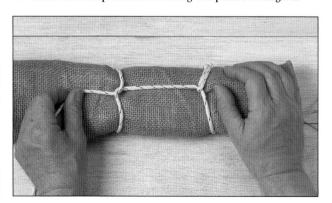

3 Pull the overhand knot tight, when, unlike mere half hitching, the extra friction will tend to hold the surrounding knot in place.

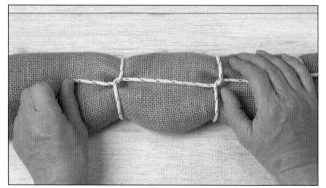

4 Add a series of such overhand knots, spaced evenly along the length of the parcel. Turn the work over and return to the starting place with a series of crossing knots and tie off.

Poldo Tackle

This all-or-nothing tensioning contrivance is quickly assembled; pull one way to tighten, the other way to slacken off. Use it for a clothes line or as a quick-release lashing for an on-deck life raft.

1 Tie a strong and secure fixed loop (an angler's loop is illustrated) in one end of the line.

2 Tuck the other end of the line through the small fixed loop to produce a large running loop.

3 Bring the end around and make a sliding bight on the running leg of the large loop.

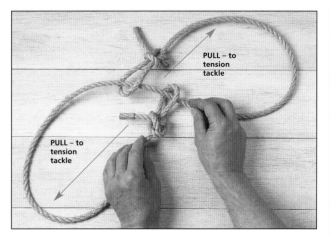

PULL – to tension tackle

PULL – to tension tackle

4 Secure the bight just made with a matching fixed loop knot. To tension the tackle, pull the two knots apart; to slacken it again, push them back together.

Chain Stitch Lashing

This lashing uses more line than many others, but it fits nicely over lumpy and bumpy long parcels, with the dividend that it can be readily undone simply by pulling on the working end. Tied in an attractive cord or string in a contrasting colour to the package, this lashing, with its pleasant zigzag effect, can be used to gift-wrap boxes and cartons, even though they may be sufficiently secure without the lashing.

1 Tie a small fixed loop in one end of the line; then pull a bight from the standing part up through it.

2 Lead the standing end away from the bight, around and up behind the object being parcelled.

3 Pull a second bight from the standing part down through the first bight already made.

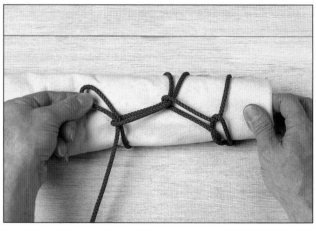

4 Lead the standing end away from the second bight, around and down behind the parcel; then pull a third bight from the standing part, up through the second bight.

5 Repeat steps 2 and 3, pulling a fourth bight down through the third bight.

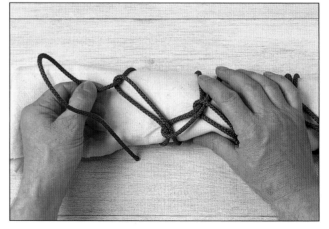

6 Continue with interlacing alternate bights until the end of the parcel is reached; pull the working end completely through the last bight.

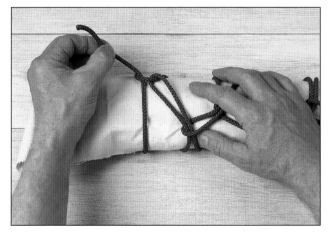

7 Lead the working end once around the almost completed parcel, prior to tucking it beneath itself.

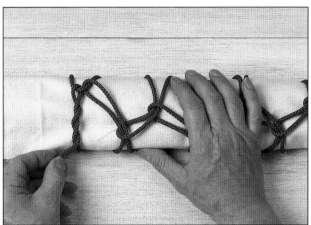

8 Finally, dog the working end around its own standing part to secure.

Diamond Hitch

Explorers, prospectors and other wilderness pioneers, dependent upon pack animals to convey all sorts of loads, once swore by this hitch, and it can still be spotted in the more authentic cowboy films. The lashing will secure irregularly shaped commodities, as they stir and strain, not only on the backs of mules and horses but also loaded on to beach buggies, snowmobiles or other motor vehicles (on or off-road). It is also ideal for human backpackers with unpackable items to carry.

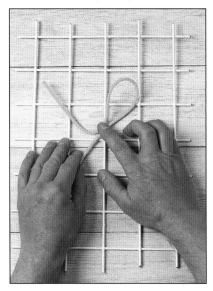

1 Select a suitable length of lashing for backpack or luggage rack.

2 Secure the standing end to a centrally placed anchorage point.

3 Take the line loosely across the load, around a second anchorage opposite the first, then return.

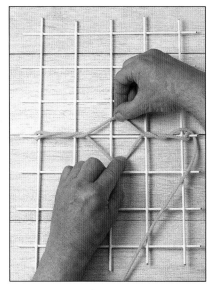

4 Twist the two parts of the lashing together, until most of the slack is removed. Find the centre of the twist.

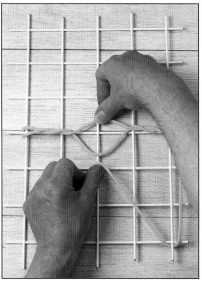

5 Lead the line down and around a corner lashing, then back to tuck centrally through the nearest centre side of the twisted portion of the lashing.

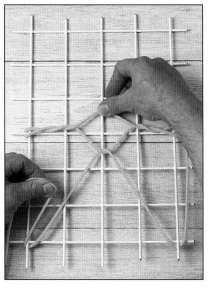

6 Take the line down around the next corner anchorage point.

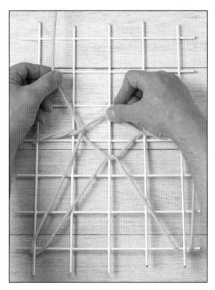

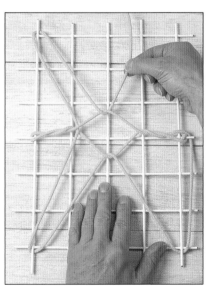

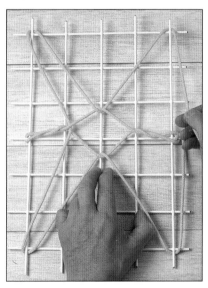

7 Then bring it up through the central diamond that gives this hitch its distinctive name.

8 Take the line around the third anchorage point and bring it back to tuck once more through the central diamond shape.

9 Lead the line around the remaining corner anchorage, and then bring it back down to the starting point. Secure it at this point.

Trucker's Hitch

Still used by truck drivers to lash down loads securely – wherever rope lashings have not been superseded by webbing straps with mechanical tensioning and locking devices – this hitch can be traced back to the carters and hawkers who once went from house to house and town to town on horse-drawn conveyances. In those days it was known as the waggoner's hitch, but its application has changed little since then.

1 Attach the lashing to an anchorage point on the far side of the vehicle or trailer, then bring it over the load to the nearside.

2 Cast an anticlockwise (counterclockwise) overhand loop in the line or lashing.

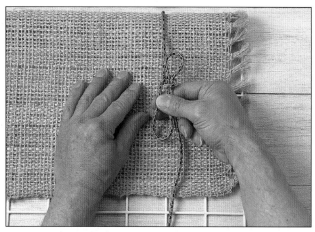

3 Make a bight in the standing part of the line and tuck it up (from the back to the front) through the pre-formed loop.

4 Impart an anticlockwise (counterclockwise) half twist to the long loop resulting from the tucked bight.

5 Add an extra half twist, creating a pair of interlocked elbows in the long lower loop.

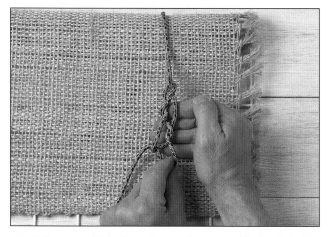

6 Pull another bight from the standing part, this time bringing it through the twisted lower loop.

7 Pass the latest lower loop over an anchorage point on the nearside of the vehicle.

8 Take the line along and lead it around another anchorage on the same side of the vehicle; then toss it over the load to the far side. Repeat steps 2–7 as often as necessary to secure the load.

Round Mat

This knotted roundel can replace an ordinary mat, or it may be glued as ornamentation or embellishment to items as diverse as a collage picture or a drum majorette's uniform.

1 Middle a length of cord and cast an anticlockwise (counterclockwise) overhand loop in the working end.

2 Bring the working end down behind the loop and arrange a symmetrical pretzel layout.

3 Pick up the other end of the cord and tuck it diagonally (up and to the left) over/under/over.

4 Lead the working end around clockwise and tuck diagonally (down and to the right) under/over/under/over.

5 Tuck the end alongside the standing part. Follow the original lead around to double or triple the knot ply. Glue or stitch the end in place on the underside.

Carrick Mat

This can be used as an actual mat, or as a component of other art and craft work. Made around the hand, the same knot can form a necktie ring.

1 Cast a clockwise overhand loop in a length of cord or rope.

2 Bring the working end down over the original loop and arrange a pretzel layout.

3 Pass the working end around (from right to left), keeping it behind the standing part.

4 Tuck it clockwise around and through the knot going over/under/over/under.

5 Tuck the working end alongside and parallel to the standing part. Follow the original lead around to double or triple the knot ply.

Ocean Plait

This good-looking design can be executed in the finest twines or the thickest ropes. Consequently it may be used as a table mat or coaster, an embellishment for bandsmen and women's uniforms, a doormat, or you might frame one and hang it on the wall. Pin thicker materials on to a cork board or polystyrene tile to keep them in place until you have made the final locking tuck.

1 Cast an anticlockwise (counter-clockwise) overhand loop in it with one end of a fairly long length of line.

2 Bend the long working end around (to the left) and lay it over the standing end of the original loop.

3 Take the end up and lay it (from left to right) over the top loop.

4 Lead the working end diagonally down (from right to left) and lay it on top of the lower loop.

5 Pick up the other half of the line – which now becomes the working end – and lay it (from left to right) over the new standing part.

6 Tuck the end diagonally (up and to the right), under/under, through the nearest loop.

7 Bring the working end around and take it diagonally from right to left over/under/over/under the knot parts.

8 Tuck the working end diagonally again (this time up from left to right), going over/under/over/under/over so that it comes out at the bottom right.

9 Tuck the working end up alongside the standing part, following the original lead around to double or triple the knot.

Long Mat

The traditional name for this is a prolong knot because the length of the mat can be extended. Given enough material (and patience), it would be possible to continue adding indefinitely to this knot. More realistically, it is used when an ocean plait is not quite long enough and needs to be enlarged.

1 Middle – more or less – a length of cord suitable for the use to which the finished mat will be put.

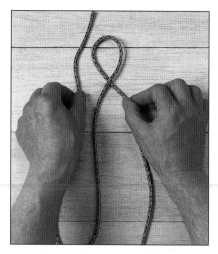

2 Cast a clockwise overhand loop and bring the working end around to create a long lefthand bight.

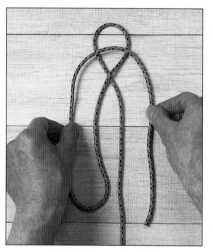

3 Lay the long working end (from left to right) over the upper bight.

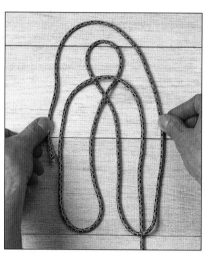

4 Taking the standing part, make a long righthand bight, on top of the previous working end, to match the lefthand bight.

5 Tuck the working end diagonally down (from right to left), over/over/under, and lay it on top of the long lefthand bight.

6 Impart a clockwise lefthand twist to the lefthand bight.

7 Impart a similar clockwise twist to the righthand long bight.

8 Lay the twisted righthand bight over the top of the twisted lefthand bight.

9 Tuck the lefthand working end diagonally (down from left to right), under/over/over/under.

10 Tuck the righthand working end diagonally (down from right to left), over/under/over/under/over.

11 Arrange the interwoven mat layout symmetrically and remove unwanted slack. Tuck the working end alongside the standing part and follow around the original lead to double or triple the mat.

Alternate Ring Hitching

Large metal rings may be hitched over to prevent them banging and clanging against hard surfaces. Smaller ones make decorative finger-holds for blind pulls, etc. Needleworkers with stamina may make dozens or hundreds of very fine ones and then stitch them together to produce lace or tatted-like wall hangings or quilts.

1 Thread a length of cord and thread it on to the ring to be covered.

2 Tie a reversed pair of half hitches, resembling a bale sling hitch.

3 Add a third half hitch, which must be the mirror-image of the second one, and pulled tight up against it.

4 Add a fourth half hitch, which must be the mirror-image of the third, and therefore the same as the second.

5 Repeat steps 2 to 4 as often as required to cover the ring completely with the cord.

Continuous Ring Hitching

This results in a slim spine and works best on rings of small cross-section.

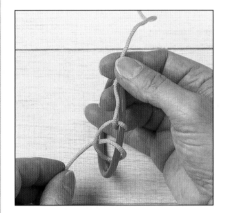

1 Tie two identical half hitches, which will resemble a clove hitch.

2 Add a third half hitch, taking care to wrap and tuck the working end in the same direction as the previous pair.

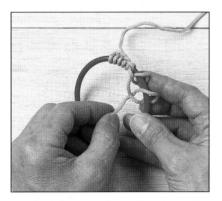

3 Straighten out the work at intervals, to ensure that the spine does not spiral around the ring; this also serves to tighten the knotting.

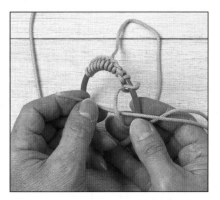

4 Continue to half hitch around the ring, always in the same direction.

5 Keep hitching and regularly straightening the spine until the ring is completely covered. The ends can be plaited, as shown in the finished picture.

Double Ring Hitching

For rings with a thicker diameter, or those made to appear so by comparatively thin cord, this version (with a rope-like spine) may look better than the continuous ring hitching. Ring hitching may be scaled up or down and applied to many handicrafts, and it can also be applied to handles.

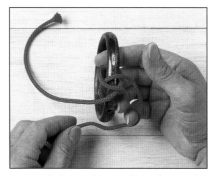

1 Lead the working end in a figure-of-eight around the ring, first going up and across the front of the ring (from left to right), then around the back (from right to left), down the front diagonally (from left to right), around the back again (right to left), tucking up at the front (left to right) and going under/over.

2 Pass the working end through the ring from right to left and then feed it through up to the right under two knot parts.

3 Repeat step 2, passing the end through the ring and again tucking up to the right beneath two knot parts.

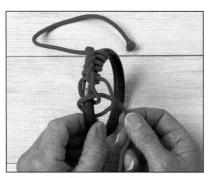

4 At intervals, straighten the spine, as it tends to drift off-centre; this also tightens the knotting.

5 Continue to wrap the working end around and through the ring, always in the same direction.

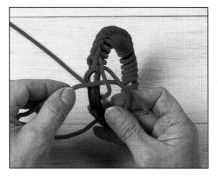

6 Repeatedly tuck up and under two cord parts, until all of the foundation of the ring is covered with the cord.

Underhand Loop Hitching

The spine that emerges from this covering is a kind of chain stitch best fitted for a thicker ring. This – and other ring hitchings – may be executed in fairly fine twines and cords by needleworkers or by rope workers in wool, cottons or silks. They are also applied with substantial leather thongs by leather workers. It is a very versatile technique. This kind of hitching looks similar to a knitting stitch, but knitted items can unravel, whereas this pattern is composed of individual knots, each of which is separately and securely tied and, unlike knitting stitches, is not reliant on the preceding knots or stitches. Use it on light pulls or curtain cords.

1 Take a turn around the ring with the cord and cross the two parts, the standing end up and the working end down.

2 Form a clockwise underhand loop with the working part of the cord.

3 Pass the working end through the ring (from right to left).

4 Tuck the end up through the underhand loop, and draw the knotting snug and tight.

5 Continue to wrap around the ring and tuck through underhand loops.

6 Reproduce the looped and tucked pattern until the ring is covered.

Ringbolt Hitching

With only a single cord, this hitching produces a spine running along the outer edge of the ring, resembling a three-strand plait or braid, making it suitable for the thickest or broadest rings.

1 Take a full turn around the ring, tucking up under two cord parts at the front, before going around again and tucking up through one part.

2 Turn the working end down and tuck diagonally (from right to left) under one knot part.

3 Wrap around the front of the ring (from left to right) and pass through the ring (from right to left).

4 Describe a figure-of-eight, diagonally up (from left to right) in front of the knotwork, then directly back (from right to left) beneath two cord parts.

5 Repeat step 4, wrapping down and to the right, through the ring (from right to left), and then up and right.

6 Then tuck the end (from right to left) under two parts. Repeat this process until the entire ring is covered with the cord.

Versatackle

Devised and published in October 1985 by George Aldridge, this tackle applies tension wherever needed. It may be tied in small cord and used as an improvised clamp for newly glued picture frames, chairs or other woodwork; in rope, it will raise heavy loads, retrieve a bogged-down motor vehicle, or it can be used to tension guylines or shrouds on tents, flagpoles or radio masts. It truly is a versatile tackle – hence its name. This device can chafe loops tied in vegetable fibre ropes, but synthetic cordage will survive much longer without weakening.

1 Make a single fixed loop in the end of the cordage (an angler's loop is ideal). At a distance somewhat greater than the two fixed points to be connected, tie a second similar loop in the bight.

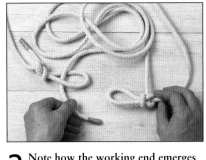

2 Note how the working end emerges from one side of the second loop; take this through the first loop from that same side.

3 Thread it through the second loop in the opposite direction.

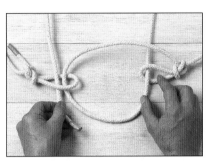

4 Circling in the same direction, pass the working end through the first loop again.

5 Pass the end through the second loop, continuing the coiling pattern.

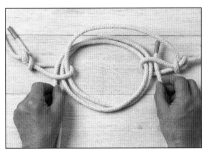

6 Take one more complete turn, so that there are three standing parts on each side of the two loops. Pull on the free end of the line to exert a powerful pull. Let go and – surprisingly – this ad hoc tackle is self-locking (but add a retaining half hitch for safety's sake). To release it, unthread the working end a tuck or two, until the entire arrangement can be loosened.

Simple Chain

This simple chain will shorten an over-long rope or cord by about one-third. It will also embellish a fine twine, to make an attractive cord to retain reading glasses, for example.

1 Cast an anticlockwise (counter-clockwise) overhand loop with a long working end.

2 Lay the working end beneath the loop and pull a bight (from back to front) through it; then pull the resulting knot tight.

3 Pull a second bight in the working end through the first bight and pull it tight.

4 Similarly, pull a third bight through the second bight and pull it tight.

5 Continue pulling, bight through bight, tightening each stage before going on to the next.

6 To finish the chain, simply tuck the working end through the preceding bight. This will secure the completed chain sufficiently.

Endless Simple Chain

This is a very neat way to join the ends of a simple chain, ensuring that it keeps the same shape even on the join. It makes an original bracelet, necklace or anklet, and it may even be used to frame a picture or mirror. The steps are illustrated in two different colours but this chain is usually made with two ends of one cord.

1 Bring the beginning and end of one or two simple chains together.

2 Tuck the final end – in this instance, the lefthand one – up through the starting loop (from the back to the front), alongside the standing end.

3 Take the working end up (from the back to the front) through its own loop, beside itself.

4 Pass the end to the right, down (from front to back) through the adjacent loop made by step 3.

5 Withdraw the standing end from the first of its tucks and replace it with the working end.

Double Chain

Known as trumpet or bugle cord (because of its use as ornamentation on military bandsmen's uniforms), this is a bulkier version of the simple chain. Work it in thick gold cord for a military look.

1 Cast two anticlockwise (counterclockwise) overhand loops, the second on top of the first.

2 Pass the long working end over the top of both loops to lie behind them.

3 Pull a bight from the working end out through both loops (from back to front).

4 Tighten a little, leaving enough slack to pull a second bight through two previous loops (from back to front).

5 Repeat step 4 as often as may be required to complete the desired length of chain.

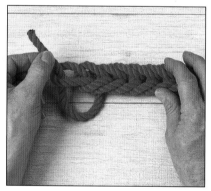

6 Finally, tuck the working end through a single loop to secure the double chain.

Endless Double Chain

Join the ends of a double chain to make a handsome body ornament or incorporate it into art and craft work. While the steps are illustrated in two different colours, for clarity, this chain is more usually made with the two ends of a single cord.

1 Bring the standing and working ends of a double chain close together.

2 Pass the working end up (from back to front) through the final loop of the standing end.

3 Tuck the end up through the knot parts beside itself (from back to front).

4 Tuck the working end down (from front to back), under one knot part, through the loop.

5 Tuck the end sideways (from top to bottom of the illustration), going over/under/over/over, as it picks up the second loop in from the standing end.

6 Lead the working end up (from back to front), going under/under, bringing it up to emerge from the third of the working end loops.

7 Finally, tuck the end down (from front to back), over/under/under, to meet up with the standing part of the line.

Braid Knot

It is possible, using this single-strand knot, to replicate the familiar three-strand pigtail plait (braid); which can then be employed to shorten rope or cord, or to decorate it. The braid knot also makes a practical makeshift handle for a suitcase or sailing dinghy daggerplate.

1 Cast a long clockwise underhand loop, with three parallel cord parts.

2 Begin the plait (braid) by bringing the righthand strand over the middle strand, to lie inside and below the lefthand strand.

3 Then take the lefthand strand over the middle strand, to lie inside and below the righthand strand.

4 Repeat step 2, noting how the outermost (furthest away) strand becomes the working one each time.

5 Repeat step 3, complying once more with the principle that the least used strand becomes the next working one.

6 Continue plaiting alternate right and lefthand strands, pulling each step tight as the work develops.

7 Untangle, by pulling out the single long working end, the loose mirror-image that inevitably accumulates during the plaiting (braiding) process.

8 Tighten and tension the plait (braid) so that one final loop remains at the end.

9 Finally, tuck the working end through the remaining loop to secure the plait (braid).

Zigzag Braid

A pair of matching strands may be shortened or made into a slip-resistant and decorative handle or lanyard by means of this simple flat braid. In coarse material (as illustrated) it makes a robust saw-tooth outline; but in finer lines it resembles a rather delicate length of tatting.

1 Bind two ropes together and, with the lefthand one, tie a half hitch around the righthand one.

2 Now tie a matching half hitch, this time with the righthand rope around the lefthand one.

3 Repeat step 1, pulling the latest half hitch snug against the preceding one.

4 Repeat step 2, pulling with an even tension to tighten the work as it develops. Continue until the braid is as long as required.

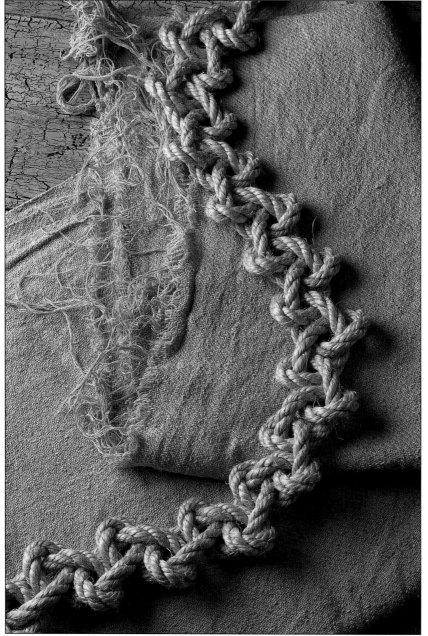

Two-Strand Braid Knot

A length of four-strand plait (braid) may be imitated, by means of this two-strand braid knot, and used to decorate lanyards. This decorative braid may be made with two cords of the same colour and type, but it is interesting to experiment with cords of two matching or contrasting colours. It can even look good if the cords are made from dissimilar materials although you will need to be extra vigilant about checking the tension of the braid as you work.

1 Middle two lengths of line and interlock the resulting bights.

2 Separate the ends of the bights a distance at least equal to the desired knot, and separate the four ends or parts into lefthand and righthand pairs.

3 Bring the outermost righthand strand across (behind) and tuck it up (from the back to the front) between the two lefthand strands.

4 Untangle the loose strands from the bight; then bring the outermost lefthand strand across (behind) and tuck it up (from the back to the front) between the two righthand strands.

5 Repeat steps 3 and 4 until the closed bight has room for just one more final tuck.

6 Tuck the next working strand through the bight to close it and secure this braid knot.

Three-Strand Braid

This is the most common type of braid. Lashings and lanyards can quickly be made from smaller stuff by this means; horses' tails or long human hair can also be made orderly with it.

1 Bind three strands together and separate them into a lefthand single strand and a righthand pair of strands.

2 Bring the outermost one of the right-hand pair across (over the front) to lie inside and below the lefthand strand.

3 Take the outermost one of the lefthand pair of strands and bring it across (over the front) to lie inside and below the righthand strand.

4 Repeat step 2, pulling and tightening the work as it develops.

5 Repeat step 3, pulling with an even tension as the work develops.

6 Repeat step 2, always taking (as the latest working strand) the one of the pair furthest away.

7 Continue plaiting (braiding) with alternate strands until the desired length is reached. Knot or bind the ends securely together to prevent them from coming undone.

Four-Strand Braid

This makes a flat lashing or
lanyard which, in stiff stuff, will
result in a detailed network of
ornamental openwork.

1 Middle two lengths of rope or cord,
looping one over the other (as
shown), and separating the four strands
into a lefthand and a righthand pair.

2 Simultaneously, cross the lefthand
pair of strands (left over right) and
the righthand pair (also left over right).

3 Then cross the innermost two
strands (right over left).

4 Repeat steps 2 and 3, with tension
and tightness to ensure a symmetrical
pattern develops.

5 Continue this process until the
desired length has been reached.
Bind the ends together.

Four-Strand Plait

Use good-quality cords to make a lead for a small dog, a lavatory or light pull, or a waist-tie for an informal garment. This is the plait (braid) that may be seen attached to the handset of vintage telephones. It may also be used to quadruple the strength of smaller cordage when no thicker cord or rope is available.

1 Bind four strands together and sub-divide them into a lefthand and a righthand pair; then take the outer one of the righthand pair across (behind), tucking it up through and between the two lefthand strands, and returning it to lie inside and below its original righthand companion.

2 Similarly, lead the outer lefthand strand around behind, to emerge between the two righthand strands, and return to lie inside and below its lefthand partner.

3 Repeat step 1, continuing to pull and tighten the paired strands as the work progresses.

4 Repeat step 2, ensuring an even tension as the work develops.

5 Continue this regular plaiting (braiding) process, with alternate outer strands, until the required length is reached. Bind the ends together.

Eight-Strand Square Plait

This chunky, herringbone weave is superb for all kinds of heavier work. Inuits (Eskimos) used it to scale up fine fishing lines for catching larger sea mammals – and today it is worked in leather thongs to make sturdy leashes for large dogs. Try different coloured strands in various positions to discover the several patterns that can be made with this plait (braid).

1 Bind eight strands together and sub-divide them into left and righthand groups of four; lead the outermost (and uppermost) lefthand strand – red, in this example – around and behind the work, to emerge in the middle of the four righthand strands, returning to lie inside and below the three companion strands back on its lefthand side.

2 Similarly, lead the outermost (and uppermost) righthand strand – green, in this instance – around behind the work, to emerge in the middle of the four lefthand strands, returning to lie inside and below its three partners back on its own righthand side.

3 Repeat step 1, being sure to take (as the working strand) the uppermost strand – that is, the one furthest away.

4 Repeat step 2, taking care to select (as the working strand) the one furthest away.

5 Continue with this process, always using (as the working strand) the one not used for the longest time.

6 Tighten the work as each step is completed; in particular, tension each strand as it goes around the unseen back of the work. Bind the ends together.

Six-Strand Round Plait

Create strong, flexible ropes with
this process, using strands of
different colours to discover the
various possible patterns. Making
this braid will be difficult at first –
but it is well worth persisting for
the striking end-product. Having
said that, children can enjoy the
various patterns that emerge
when different coloured strands
are used to make this plait.

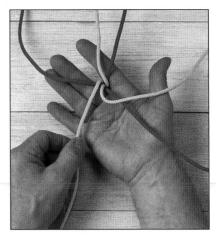

1 Seize six strands, three of one colour alternately spaced between three of another (or, if all are of one colour, then mark the end of every other one with a felt-tipped pen).

2 Turn each yellow strand – in this example – down anticlockwise (counterclockwise), over the adjacent red strand.

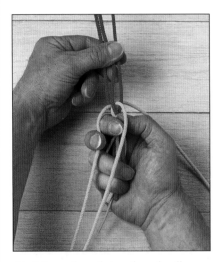

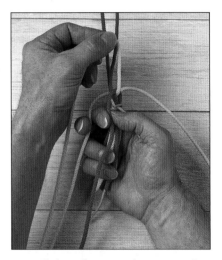

3 Lift up the red strands and pull down evenly on each yellow strand in turn.

4 Turn one of the red strands down (clockwise) over the top of its adjacent yellow strand.

5 Lift the yellow strand up to contain and hold the turned-down red one.

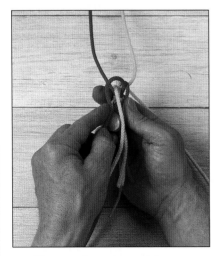

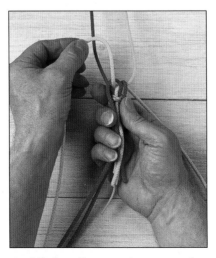

6 Turn another red strand down (clockwise) over the top of its adjacent yellow strand.

7 Lift the yellow strand up to contain and hold this second turned-down red one.

8 Turn the remaining red strand down over the top of the last of the yellow strands.

9 Lift the third of the yellow strands up to join the other two.

10 Repeat this trio of paired movements – one strand going down, the other coming up – until the desired length of plait (braid) is achieved.

Glossary

ABSEIL A climber's self-controlled descent of an anchored – and often retrievable – climbing rope.
ANCHORAGE Boating – a general term that refers to moorings and the bending of cordage (by means of hitches) to various attachments; climbing – a safe belaying point.
ARAMIDES The first commercial manmade (synthetic) fibres do not melt when heated. Their high cost limits them to specialized applications.
BARREL KNOT see Blood Knot.
BELAY Boating – to make fast to a cleat or pin, often with a round turn followed by a figure-of-eight (or two) and then another round turn; climbing – the method of securing a climber in case of a fall.
BEND A name given to any one of the knots that bind (bend) two separate ropes together.
BIGHT A slack part of rope or other cordage between the two ends, particularly when it forms a partial loop.
BLOOD KNOT Any one of the strong and secure knots that depend upon numerous wrapping turns, favoured by anglers, cavers and climbers. (The name is derived from a limited surgical use.)
BRAID A term generally interchangeable with plait; but one that is sometimes stated to refer only to strands interwoven to make a flat pattern. (See also Plait.)
BREAKING STRENGTH The manufacturer's estimation of the load a rope will bear before it ruptures, expressed in kilograms and tonnes, taking no account of wear and tear, shock loading or knots that may reduce the figure drastically. (See also Safe Working Load.)
CABLE Strictly speaking, three righthanded hawsers (laid up lefthanded) make a nine-strand cable; but the term may also be loosely applied to any large length of rope.

CAPSIZE What occurs when a knot layout is distorted due to overloading, misuse or careless tightening. It may also be done deliberately as a means of quick release.
CARABINER See Karabiner.
CORD Small stuff under 10 mm/5⁄12 in diameter.
CORE Fibres, yarns and laid or braided materials that inertly fill the unwanted space at the heart of a four (or more) strand rope, or that actively contribute desirable qualities, such as strength or elasticity to sheath-and-core ropes.
DOG To improvise a temporary running eye by making a bight in the working end of cord, around its own standing part, and then tucking the end several times to trap it in place.
EFFICIENCY The actual strength of a knot in a rope or cord, expressed as a percentage of its theoretical breaking strength.
ELBOW Two crossing points created by an extra twist in a loop.

EYE A small round loop.
FIBRE The smallest element in all vegetable rope and cordage.
FILAMENT See Monofilament.
FRAY The accidental or deliberate unlaying of a rope's end to its component strands, yarns and fibres, multi- or monofilaments.
HARD LAID Stiff cordage.
HAWSER Any three-strand rope.
HEART See Core.
HITCH Any knot used to make a line fast to an anchorage such as a rail, spar, post, ring or another rope.
KARABINER A D-shaped or pear-shaped metal snap-ring, with a pivoting gate that can be securely closed, used by cavers and climbers.
KERNMANTEL Climbing rope construction consisting of a core (or kern), often of parallel bunches of fibres contained within a tightly woven protective sheath.
KINK A damaging deformation caused by an over-tight loop.
KNOT The term for stoppers, loops and self-sufficient bindings (thus excluding bends or hitches); also the generic word for all rope and cordage tucks and ties.
LANYARD A short length of cord that is used to lash, secure or suspend an object.
LAY The direction in which rope strands spiral as they go away from from the viewer, either clockwise (righthanded, Z-laid) or anticlockwise/counterclockwise (lefthanded, S-laid).
LEAD (Pronounced "leed") The direction taken by the working end as it goes around or through an object or knot.
LINE Any rope with a specific function (for example, a tow line or washing line).
LOCKING TUCK The concluding lead of a working end that secures any knot in its finished form, without which it would unravel or collapse.
LOOP A bight with a crossing point.

MAKE FAST To attach a line to an anchorage or belay (often with a hitch).
MESSENGER The name for a throwing or heaving line when it is used to pull a thicker cord or rope across an intervening space.
MIDDLE Used as a verb, to double a rope or cord so as to locate its centre.
MONOFILAMENT Continuous synthetic fibre of uniform diameter and circular cross-section larger than 50 micons/1⁄500 in. (See also Multifilament.)
MULTIFILAMENT Very fine continuous synthetic fibre of uniform diameter and circular cross section less than 50 microns/1⁄500 in. (See also Monofilament.)
NATURAL FIBRE Processed plant products used to make rope and other cordage.
NIP The point within a knot where friction may be concentrated.
NOOSE A free-running, sliding or adjustable loop.
NYLON The first synthetic (manmade) fibre of merit available to the cordage industry. There are two grades: Nylon 66 is extensively used in the UK and USA; Nylon 6 (made available under trade names such as Perlon and Enkalon) is widely used in Europe and Japan, as well as being available in the UK and USA.
OVERHAND LOOP A loop (clockwise or anticlockwise/counterclockwise) in which the working end is laid on top of the standing part. (See also Loop.)
PLAIT A term generally interchangeable with braid, but which can refer only to interwoven strands forming a pattern that is three-dimensional in cross-section. (See also Braid.)
POLYESTER A widely used synthetic cordage (trade names Dacron and Terylene).
POLYETHYLENE A polyolefin synthetic (manmade) fibre (commonly known as Polythene/plastic).

POLYPROPYLENE A versatile polyolefin synthetic fibre.
PRUSIKING To climb a rope using a knot that jams when downward pressure is applied but can slide up the rope when the weight is removed.
RAPPEL See Abseil.
REEF Boating – to reduce sail area in strong winds (verb); each individual fold or roll of sail taken in (noun).
ROPE Cordage over 10 mm/5⁄12 in in diameter.
ROUND TURN In which a working end completely encircles a ring, rail, post or rope, and finishes up alongside its own standing part. (See also Turn.)
S-LAID Lefthanded (anticlockwise/counterclockwise).
SAFE WORKING LOAD The estimated load a rope may withstand, taking into account various weakening factors (wear and tear, damage, effect of knots and other uses); it may be as little as one-seventh the quoted breaking strength. (See Breaking Strength.)

SECURITY The integral stability of a knot.
SLING An endless rope or webbing (tape) band or strop.
SMALL STUFF A casual term for any cordage, not rope.
SOFT LAID Any flexible rope and cordage.
SPLIT FILM Synthetic (manmade), ribbon-like fibres produced from a plastic sheet.
STANDING END The inactive end of cord. (See also Working End.)
STANDING PART That part of a rope or cord anywhere between working and standing ends.
STAPLE FIBRES Graded natural fibres of limited length and strength, due to their plant origins; also discontinuous synthetic (manmade) fibres created by cutting filaments into discrete lengths.
STRAND The largest element of a rope, made from contra-twisted yarns.
STRENGTH The integral ability of knotted cordage to withstand a load.
STRING Relatively cheap and disposable small cord and twine.
STROP See Sling.
SYNTHETIC ROPE Cordage that is made from synthetic (manmade) multifilaments, monofilaments, staple fibres or split film.
TAG END Angling – working end.
THIMBLE A metal or plastic lining for an eye.
THREAD Fine line.
TURN A 360 degree wrap around a rig, rail, post or rope. (See also Round Turn.)
UNDERHAND LOOP A loop in which the working end is laid beneath the standing part.
WHIPPING A binding to prevent a rope's end from fraying.
WORKING END The active end of a rope or cord. (See also Standing End.)
YARN The basic element of rope strands, spun from natural fibres or synthetic (manmade) materials.
Z-LAID Righthanded (clockwise).

Index

Further Information

SUPPLIERS

English Braids, Spring Lane, Malvern WR14 1AL
Tel: 01684 892 222
Fax: 01684 892 111
Their marine sales division caters for the recreational sector and sail boat racing. Suppliers of barrier ropes, starter cords, shock cords, whipping twines, webbing and web-lash securing systems, and stainless steel hollow fids. Contact them for the location of your nearest stockist.

Eurorope Limited, 4 Phoenix Court, Atkinson Way, Foxhills Industrial Estate, Scunthorpe DN15 8QJ
Tel: 01724 280 480
Fax: 01724 857 750
Wholesale suppliers of rope, cord, twines, nets, lifting gear slings and accessories. Contact them for the location of your nearest stockist.

Des & Liz Pawson, Footrope Knots, 501 Wherstead Road, Ipswich, Suffolk IP2 8LL
Tel: 01473 690 090
Suppliers of traditional rope, cordage and smaller stuff; wire rope and chain; canvas; tools; fittings; fenders, knotboards, chest beckets and other knotwork; books (new, secondhand and rare). Their unique ropework museum may be visited free (by prior arrangement).

Kevin Keatley, K.J.K. Ropeworks, Town Living Farmhouse, Puddington, Tiverton, Devon EX16 8LW
Tel/fax: 01884 860 692
Supplier of cords and fittings, especially braided synthetics. Price list on request.

Leanda, 39 Borrowdale Drive, Norwich, Norfolk NR1 4LY
Tel/fax: 01603 434 707
Textile craft equipment manufacturers; specialists in Japanese-style braiding and passementerie equipment; accessories for spinning and weaving; also a book list.

Marlow Ropes Ltd, Diplocks Way, Hailsham, East Sussex BN27 3JS
Tel: 01323 847 234
Fax: 01323 440 093
email: yachting@marlow ropes.com
Website: http://www.marlow ropes.com
Market leaders in yacht rope technology and such accessories as shockcord, barrier ropes, toestrap and buoyancy bag webbing, whipping twine, splicing kits, sail repair tapes.

Ann Norman, Sagaman, Aston Road, Bampton, Oxfordshire, OX18 2AL
Tel/fax: 01993 850 823
email: sagaman@compuserve.com
Designer, handweaver and maker of cords, including four-strand cords, and ropes of traditional laid structure. Advice offered and commissions accepted.

Oakhurst Quality Products Limited, Warsop Trading Estate, Hever Road, Edenbridge, Kent TN8 5LD
Tel: 01732 866 668
Fax: 01732 864 555
Wholesale suppliers of rope, twine, cordage, chain, doormats, work gloves, garden sundries. Contact Brenda Risdon for the location of your nearest stockist.

BIBLIOGRAPHY

Asher, Harry, *The Alternative Knot Book* (Nautical Books, A. & C. Black, London, 1989)
Ashley, Clifford Warren, *The Book of Knots* (Doubleday, New York, 1944/Faber & Faber, London, 1947)
Bailey, Hazel, *Knotting for Guides* (Girl Guides Association, London, 1987)
Chisnall, Robert (Editor), *Rock Climbing Safety Manual* (Ontario Rock Climbing Association, Canada, 1984)
Day, Cyrus Lawrence, *Quipus & Witches' Knots* (University of Kansas Press, 1967)
Graumont, Raoul, and Hensel, John, *The Encyclopaedia of Knots and Fancy Rope Work* (Cornell Maritime Press, Cambridge, Maryland, 1939)
Graves, Richard H., *The Bushcraft Handbooks* (Graves, Sydney, 1952)
Griend, P. van de, and Turner, J.C. (eds), *The History and Science of Knots* (World Scientific Publishing Company, Singapore, New Jersey, London, Hong Kong, 1996)
I.G.K.T., *Knotting Matters* (1982 to the present)
Kreh, Lefty, and Sosin, Mark, *Practical Fishing & Boating Knots* (A. & C. Black, London, 1975)
Luebben, Craig, *Knots for Climbers* (Chockstone Press, Evergreen, Colorado, 1993)
March, Bill, *Mountain Rope Techniques* (Cicerone Press, Cumbria, 1983)
Noonan, Michael, *Climbing Knots – for Lefties and Righties* (I.C.S. Books, Merryville, Indiana, 1997)
Padgett, Allen, & Smith, Bruce, *On Rope* (National Speliological Society, Huntsville, Alabama, 1992)
Payne, Lee and Bob, "The Forgotten Zeppelin Knot" (*Boating Magazine*, March 1976)
Perkins, Andy, Tapes, *Slings & Harnesses* (Troll Safety Equipment, 1991)
Rosenow, Frank, *Seagoing Knots* (W.W. Norton, New York, 1990)
Shaw, George Russell, *Knots – Useful & Ornamental* (Bonanza Books, New York, 1924 and 1933)
Spencer, Charles L., *Knots, Splices & Fancy Work* (Brown, Son & Fergusson, Glasgow, 1934)
Sweet, John, *Scout Pioneering* (Scout Association, London, 1974)
Toss, Brion, *The Rigger's Apprentice* International Marine Publishing Co, Camden, Maine, 1984)
Trower, Nola, *Knots and Ropework* (Helmsman Books, Marlborough, Wiltshire, 1992)
Vare, Alan B., *The Hardy Book of Fisherman's Knots* (Camden Publishing, London, 1987)
Warner, Charles, *A Fresh Approach to Knotting and Ropework* (Warner, Yanderra, NSW, 1992)

ACKNOWLEDGEMENTS

The author is indebted to David Ierston, marine sales manager for English Braids Ltd, who supplied superb cordage for this book.

The following, from whom the cordage was obtained to tie most of the specimen knots illustrated, were also generous with their time and advice: Brenda Risdon (Oakhurst Quality Products Ltd.); Kevin Keatley (K.J.K. Ropeworks); James Martin (Marlow Ropes Ltd.); Des & Liz Pawson (Footrope Knots).

A special extra acknowledgement is due to Des Pawson who, by allowing access to his home and workplace, made possible the unique portraits of traditional ropework that enrich this book.

ORGANIZATIONS

The International Guild of Knot Tyers was established in 1982 and now has a worldwide membership. It is a registered educational charity, dedicated to preserving and promoting the art, craft and science of knots.

Anyone – expert or novice – interested in tying knots may join. IGKT members enjoy a quarterly magazine, *Knotting Matters,* in addition to regular meetings. For more details and an application form, contact:

David Walker
IGKT Hon Secretary
PO Box 3540
Chester, CH1 9FE
tel: +44 (0)1244 682117
email: dwfenders@yahoo.co.uk

(Knotting can also be found on the Internet.)